The Red Tower

The Red Tower

New & Selected Poems

☾

DAVID RIGSBEE

NEWSOUTH BOOKS
Montgomery | Louisville

NewSouth Books
105 S. Court Street
Montgomery, AL 36104

Library of Congress Cataloging-in-Publication Data

Rigsbee, David.
The red tower : new & selected poems / David Rigsbee.
p. cm.
ISBN-13: 978-1-58838-231-3
ISBN-10: 1-58838-231-1
I. Title.
PS3568.I375R43 2010
813'.54—dc22

2010013314

Design by Randall Williams
Printed in the United States of America

ACKNOWLEDGMENTS

The Adirondack Review, The American Poetry Review, Aspen Leaves, Birmingham Review, Birdsuit (U. K.), *The Brooklyn Rail, Café Solo, Cairn, The Carolina Quarterly, Cimarron Review, The Cortland Review, Exquisite Corpse, The Fiddlehead* (Canada), *The Florida Review, The Georgia Review, The Greensboro Review, Hayden's Ferry Review, Inertia Magazine, Ironwood, The Journal, The Literary Review, The Manhattan Review, The Marlboro Review, The New Orleans Review, The New Yorker, The North Atlantic Review, The Ohio Review, Poetry, The St. Andrews Review, The Sewanee Review, Simple Vows, Solo, The South Carolina Review, The Southern Humanities Review, The Southern Review, Sulphur River Review, The Texas Review, VerseDaily, The Western Humanities Review, The William and Mary Review, Willow Springs.*

FOR JILL AND MAKAIYA

Contents

I. New Poems

Harp

A bad painting, at once aggressive and shy,
connects its glassy, Alpine blue
with a utilitarian sofa beneath—where no one sits—
and that in turn to footstools
like toadstools leading away, becoming flagstones
that would take the eye the distance
across the domestic space of the room.
Leaves wobble by the window opening
and across from that window
on the fifth story balcony above the sidewalk
(where immigrants drift in shoots and eddies)
a young, bespectacled mother puts out the wash:
blouses and leggings on metal dowels,
underwear in an aluminum rack tub.
She disappears and returns with an armload
of baby wash, though where this will go,
now that the racks are full, is not clear.
But distribute them she will,
paying no mind to the encroaching garden
from the balcony above, nor the slag
of toys piled on the balcony below.
Nor of me, sitting by a wooden harp, in a room
not mine, thinking of hot, loser towns
where I am no longer, of years imagined
when I never was. One child's dress, an ever-
serviceable blue cotton smock, says it all,

hanging four-square from the balcony rail,
as if in the absence of its little owner, billowing,
it took that absence on a journey.
Pointless speculation, says a contrapuntal voice,
and yet that is what I did with my life.

After Reading

I put down the book thinking
how purity is a curse, how it
puts us off the human
for whom it better fits
to turn away from the shore
in favor of the garbage and the grief.
I remember standing in the nave of St. Peter's
looking at the smooth, dead body of Christ
held in Mary's arms and secretly admiring
the madman whose hammer
chipped the same marble that made
Michaelangelo such a monster.

The Red Tower

For two years I drove by a mountain
and wondered how long it would take
to tunnel through using a teaspoon.
That's how dead my brother was.
No, more. And I thought the young
Yeats was wrong when he wrote
that God talked to those long dead.
I imagined a blinking tower
on a mountain: the red light pulsed
but raised no one. Because even if
God talked to the dead, what could
He possibly say to them?
What could He possibly say?

The Apartment

Through the window I saw, in a canted plane,
an apartment building rise—stonework, ironwork
and detailing where every other window
becomes a recessed balcony. The penultimate
floor bore an ironwork cincture, and I was reminded
of my vertigo stepping out from the top
of Trajan's Tower in Rome years ago.
The guardrail stopped at knee-level,
and the tower floor itself did not exceed
three-feet wide. At your back, granite;
out beyond the eyes: air's abyss. Now,
a convenience store occupied street level,
but the air was a void all the same.
A sculptor, on commission, carved the spiral
of the Emperor's conquests among the Etruscans,
the Dacians, and the Goths—like all killing
utterly repetitious in the ringing iron,
the screams of horses, the helmeted bodies.
At some point, the eyes following the spiral
could no longer take in the scope of victory,
but the vanishing point was no less bloody
than the start, the swords no less blunt.
By contrast, the top floor I saw—tilted
and tiled—had only a rail and no place
out from the window to stand upon. Already
the windows on either side were indistinguishable

from skylights. Who stood at that rail
saw boulevards stretching all the way
to the inhospitable suburbs. Just so,
saints were said to emerge from their cells
and pause, before going forth out of the spirit,
in their rope belts, into the stony forests.

Mink

"Time can render true what began in falsehood."
—DAVID DOWNIE

We passed on Mink DeVille and went down
to another club where studded, junkie coxcombs
leaned against old brick, profiled Mohawks
like halos in Fra Angelico, at maximum extension.
We bumped and snorted, then met the dawn
glazed with dew, under the bridge, immortal.

Last night, I lay awake listening
to summer's revelers hooting drunkenly,
occasionally rising to fisticuffs—until light
crawled across the ceiling. Then, following
a moratorium hour, came the sound
of street cleaners scrubbing stone.

My own mother demonstrated how gasps
displaced breath until entropic muscle
ironed a vanishing point's V into a flat-line.
A poet friend gave my old inamorata
six to seven years to live, max. I saw us
staggering around the Village, brains ablaze,

swearing to hold our last meeting
in the same grave. Or so she said in a bar.

Those words, privileged, defiant, false,
also spaced themselves from previous words
until they fell silent—between us, I mean.
We met in a grave of words

but my fantasy kept a conversation
going about high and distant things.
That conversation gave shape to the eruption
of drunks howling on the pavement below
as they waited for the sweepers and the first
men in suits headed for the subway.

At the same time that spirit's rendition
of sweet nothings slobbered into the ear of a god,
I moved at the heart of a deep reverie.
The times between being all ordinary saviors
needed to hail souls to 2.0, I couldn't help
noticing the smell of water on stone

and thought of Auden's face, the penitent
carved from the young man, the way a teardrop,
advancing from its source, stains the almanac.

A Life Preserver

He watches the light move in and out
behind the evening clouds and listens
to the wild duck's long, sad cadence,
interrupted by crows. He senses
the still air is indifferent
to these rituals. For all that,
he knows the connections there
are the nodes of moments
already deep in the braid
of a rope, coiled and put
in a public place under lock and key,
a life preserver, in case of emergency.

Russians

It wasn't the end when
my girlfriend handed me the phone
in the middle of the night and said,
"Here. Say hello to my husband."
And it wasn't the end of anything
when another grabbed the wheel at 70
and screamed, "I could pull this
right off the road right now!
I could do it *right now!*"
Those frenzies have passed
into something like the memory
of a good novel, weighted in one's lap
when the day is cleared,
and there's nothing left to do
but look in on the Russians
passing out at the feet of their superiors,
emptying their wallets into the fireplace,
throwing their brain-stuffed heads
before the locomotive of History,
rather than face the vivid memory
of errors committed when the face
was hot and stared into the eyes
of that intransigent, that other face.

The Ferry

There doesn't seem much point in following
the ridge that trails off until the cloud
absorbs the rock. I had been trying
to make an image for that change,
how the hawk merges with the bare madrona,
how the slap of the motorboat hull
is followed by the long, rolling wake.
After lunging repeatedly, each in choke-chain,
porch dogs thought the better of it
and rounded their day with a sleep.
A crow came toward me on a road
as if I were no longer wild.
The ferry plowed on without a variation
and I felt almost formal in its transit,
almost a man finally in compliance
with orders send down long ago.

Rorty

Raised by Trotskyites, he had a soft spot
for the writerly reactionaries: Eliot,
Larkin, poets steeped in Original Sin,
for whom poetry was the *scala sanctorum*
and the best lines ineffable.
Not for him, the abolisher of Truth,
the materialism of words. He loved
not only what they could do, but what they
aspired to do. One day, setting
down his bourbon after a seminar meant
to engage unkempt, querulous supernerds,
he told me that Allen Tate had been his
favorite teacher at the U. of Chicago.
Grinning, he told how each class
consisted of Tate reciting a single poem,
in his sonorous, waterlogged baritone,
then pausing, adding, "Isn't that beautiful?"

School of the Americas

I forgave my aunt for boasting she knew
Lt. Calley and for banishing her daughter
to a home for the unwed at nineteen
(finishing school in Florida, we heard).
The girl, now nearing middle age, would be
somewhere in America. Where?
New facts assert their traction
now that our relatives have died off
and left the home stretch unimpeded
by their last emergencies. What I couldn't
forgive was the time my aunt woke my brother
and gripping him by the forelock
hissed he was "stupid" to have kicked
my uncle, a full colonel, the day before,
as he made ready to leave for his job
with the infamous School of the Americas,
where he taught history to killers. He said
nothing, but the look of military hauteur
made us regret our vacation there.
In those hot days I pursued my cousin,
who had already added boys to her résumé.
My brother moped and never seemed
as animated by mischief again.
My uncle took his pension by an Arnold
Palmer course near the base,
a retired general on the far side

of the water trap. I couldn't forgive
whatever it was that planted the cruelty
in her voice—or my uncle's silence.
But the butterfly effect, secret timing,
and indirection spread and toughened
death's vine. If to forgive is to
bring back to life, let them lie
in the peace of mistaken privilege,
if peace it is. As for me, I can't
and I don't. Let death be the lesson
again, as it was in the beginning,
so that what it is without them
unfolds in love's stead, under the sky
where I lie back, eyes open, breathing.

Gil's Sentence

"Gil Scott-Heron To Be Sentenced."
— *New York Times*, JULY 7, 2006

"I find that rhetoric does my thinking for me,"
she said, flipping the page, moving on,
having out-Plathed Plath, including
the bitchy conjurations of voice
that threatened to make all a trick
and fostered ill will. Next up, me.
I read my serious, inadequate verse
and recalled the assassinating queries
of my undergraduate workshops:
"What is the function of the ego in this poem?"
"What does the third person mediate? Or is it
really you?" So often the poem came down
to *you*, and after my soft-voiced rendition,
silence followed suit, a reset button
before the class critic trained an interrogating
eye on one offending line. Elliott Coleman,
too aged and amiable to rein in
the revolutionary spirits of the seminar
pretended a real point of craft was at issue
and let the *sans-coulottes* have their way.
"It's sentimental," said one. "The subject
is unstable," said another. I had
no answer to these questions and sat

silently, a you, while the rest of the eyes
wobbled back and forth as if not quite
believing their luck in having stumbled
on a massacre. Then a large black man rose,
I mean actually stood up and in doing so
tipped over his unlocked briefcase
spilling old cups, record albums, a copy
of his recent (published) novel and some spoons.
Scanning the table, he who had been silent
all semester debuted a serrated baritone
that wondered about the merit of intention,
something he thought neglected ("Intention is
the moon I follow," I seem to remember
his saying, though the verbatim trips here).
He was risen to that defense when justice
was poetic and of course snubbed me
later when I tried to ingratiate myself
with a lame joke in our apartment elevator.
That other was about language: that was all.
But this was the weekend. He was in his
other world with his band, his other means.
Four or five menacing Afros with shades
followed him silently up to a different view
of that white moon out in the alley,
beyond my place, beyond where I got off.

Roofers

At the knock and sound of my name
I would rise and sit before my father's meal—
fried eggs, grits, link sausage, canned
biscuits—watching him pore over,
then fold, the *Morning Herald* by his place.
In the still dark we would cross town
in an old Chevy, pick up a man
by name of Whitey or Buck,
and we would sit, three to the bench,
through lightless streets to an old house
below Forest Hills, or some mill-hand's place,
hard against Duke Forest.
Pretty soon, we were roofing, gouging off
the outdated, loose, and rotted shingles,
flinging them over the dark edge,
laying down new ones in tight array,
nail-lined, error-free. We woke
the neighborhoods those Saturdays.
Hammers in holster, we stood in the midst
of rooftops as the colors came on,
first the long-ago rose, then a strange green
as my father, turning, bent to his row
and one by one, from between
his silent lips, pulled the nails.

Theology

Downstairs I hear Jill on the phone
with the oncologist. They could be
discussing theology or how to keep the strike
going without breaking the company.
After all, whole neighborhoods,
like unsecured cargo, know the rough slide
from rail to rail. She laughs

and I take it the doctor, a cautious young man,
stands momentarily in the ray
that shoots down from an opening
in the cloud cover.
Perhaps they shared a joke about age,
that party boat steaming westward
where the sun, always setting,
pokes through here and there looking,
as it were, for daylight.

Wild ducks below skim off across the sound.
Their cries answer the question
I would have put to the man,
but I see where they're going with this
and the thing, animal to animal,
they carry into the weather.

In Ohio

Dick made the point about Hegel:
"If he had said of the System,
'but after all, it was only a joke,'
he would have been the greatest philosopher
who ever lived. Instead,
he said that was the way it really was—the truth."
Crossing the Ohio, I felt the air change.
SUVs appeared in the rearview mirror.
Many pulled past at that point,
their cherry taillights streaking ahead.
It was December. They wanted to get home.
If my brother had written
it was all a joke, my life,
before the bullet cored out his wits,
it would have been a death
worthy of a philosopher.
Instead, he said how sorry he was—
that crushing life, the guilt
before parents and God, the secrets
that left his soft parrot mute,
while the first snow-plows rumbled by,
lights swiveling, the iron blades
lowering into place.

Thinking about Logan

I marveled at Logan's late poem
celebrating the bride of his youth,
the fiery anticipation and shyness
with which they stared at each other's rings,
before crossing the river, hills rising before them.
The future, which has the advantage
over a poet's love, manages to beckon
with the silvery twist of a treetop
as fall arrives, in garish and particular ways:
sunlight glaring off the dust of windshields
without, the oily grime of breath within,
dust in the tobacco leaves drooping
where the reaper comes, an Hispanic worker
perched on the driver's seat, itself leaning out
over the soil like Democritus' lantern.
When asked who I wanted to see
when I first visited Frisco, I said,
"Logan." My teacher said, 'Oh, no, you don't.
He's foraging garbage cans in the Castro,
a bum." Outed and drunk, he stood
there at the finale of a festival not
many years before. And not many before that
found a new image for Jesus's cross-mate,
nailed to time on Cabrini Green. I had
my own first wife to dazzle the new man
I was, and I knew the human thrill

of those first rings, before the animal snapped
and the brain slid to the back of the skull;
before the heart on derelict pilgrimage
could put two garbage can morsels together.
I didn't see him then, and not long after,
he was gone. What followed coarse fact was
the gradual blurring of detail, followed in its turn
by forgetting altogether (my students, for instance
draw a blank). But I remember the shiver
he wrote about, that passion holding desire
between the zig of attraction and the zag of doubt,
the young husband offering his face to that
of the girl, who looked up from the ring, not
finding anywhere the stranger they were to meet.

Holding Lear

To his children, the father sent a note:
"Henceforth, all requests for gifts and loans
should be made through my attorney."
A coin dropped under the table first rolls,
then wobbles in an onrush of uncertainty
until it lies down spinning, speeding up
even as it settles, before coming to rest
altogether, an inert thing among things.
When it was a wheel, it dreamed
the Royal Brougham was dead weight
without it, the government in ruins.
In seeming sympathy I lie dreaming,
the inertial force real as a foot-stopper,
familiar as a cat, while downstairs
my daughter looks out to sea by staring
into her compact. When it was clear
he was dying, my father who hugged a pillow
months to his aching lung, cut loose
and cried in the night like a girl.
Standing in Barnes & Noble, I reread
the opening lines of *King Lear*, "I thought
the king had more affected . . ." and put
it down, the Arden edition with its
massive apparatus, the text afloat
on an ocean of explanatory notes,
and on the cover, a bare tree crooking

charcoal joints, leaves long in the process
of blowing out over bare earth, a fact
not even bad art can fail to get right.

II. Selected Poems

Equinox

A slow burn. And then, even the cells
whisper goodbye in a slow, vegetal loneliness.
Today the stem goes to a stump, a seam
along which the leaf is cloven and rains
down in this rain. If the separation
defines the kiss, I have seen so many
falling out of love today

that little remains except imagining the stretch
between the ground and the crooked corn,
a simple magic. For miles
the orchards shrink to gristle and joint
and propose to carry the white load of sleep
like watchmen in the knife factory.

It is the equinox, and today I feel
the thrall that reconciles the animal
and the hole, cloud and lake, the sexes.
The ticking at the window grows: the odorless rain,
but in the kitchen the summer flies still swirl.
I hunt them all, as if nothing
should learn to expect the impossible.

Negative eloquence, it has all returned,
if deep withdrawal is the return to self,
is why the fire saves nothing, discards nothing

and old blood shifts from red to black,
why maple ignites like jelly in the frost,
root, trunk, branch, and here, your leaf.

A Respectable Man

(Tolstoy's Notebook)

I didn't sleep well and got up
and wrote about bravery. And so I forgot
to sit and reflect on the muzhiks.
This morning I looked frequently

in the mirror (only a ludicrous thing
can come of this!), but I was happy
nonetheless with the deception and so
snuggled back into bed with a book.

From now on, in order to amend my affairs
I must daily inspect my stupidity
in person, so to speak; stop building castles
in the air and disdaining the forms

adopted by all other people but me.
Accordingly I made rules: constantly force
your mind to act with all its possible strength.
That is Rule 1. The second follows:

What you've decided to do, do well,
and do no matter what. And the corollaries:
think over every order for the management
of the estate. No retreat from reality

permitted! If need be, be cold and flat,
but only after close scrutiny
and dire necessity. At parties
dance with the most important ladies.

Speak distinctly, but offer no impressions
you will have to live up to next time
in society. Choose difficult positions
and be foursquare in front of onlookers.

Try both to begin and end the conversation
always, but without habitual arguing
and constant switching from Russian to French.
Act! And carry on despite confusion.

Seek out the company of people
higher than yourself, for they harmonize
with the sphere of the possible, and theirs
is an ease that time strangely sweetens.

Thus the key will be to draw a map
in advance for a day, a month, a whole
life, and as many days as I can be true
to my resolve I will continue to set myself

in advance. I must always know
at rigid intersections of time and place
how long I will stay and with what
to concern myself, Doubtless most

of these resolutions will be altered,
but all alternations must be explained
in the notebook, whose useful goal is
that I must rise after, and be something.

As for you, I know you'll never believe
that I can change. You'll say, "So,
still at zero!" No, this time
I'll change in an entirely different way.

Before, I would mumble to myself,
"Now, let's do something," and sink.
But this time, God willing, I will
change, and someday be a respectable man.

The Stone House

i.m. Edmund Wilson

Many times I watched from that window
over a jimmied desk and saw how,
undiminished by the season, the starlings
dived from invisibility to a crevice in the wall.
The lesson was, ferocity in smallness.
This I take from your text,
none of mine. Sometimes even the Muses
stack in the tall sky like jets.

As in Joseph Cornell, every window
boxed a moment, and time stared in
from drumlin and elm, as you stared out.
But upstairs, it was mostly azure,
darting birds and clouds—
a perspective for iconoclasts—
sometimes including rain. Is this what
you saw, who came down, and died?

Wanted: a sky-blue life,
wild valleys brought to heel
by threshers and the queer tame men
walking the swath of a glacier.
Wanted too, a meaning for these footsteps,
these crawfish on the stone ledge, crawling
back to the river, and the tiny water-shrew

there, particular and bashful.

Once a cat on tiptoe crossed
the windowsill at midnight
crying as though in possession
of a human word it wanted
desperately to express. Stepping
outside, I found gray quills
like frozen breath lying on the lawn.
You were two years in the earth.

That night in a dream I heard
slipper-steps by the door.
I rose and floated down the stairs
to a great ball and danced to sleep
again, later waking at the bird hour,
the calls flying heavily over the fields.
Is this what you saw: this blue morning
at the end of night, the end?

I too wanted—but that's nothing
to a ghost. One evening
I dragged a fireplace log in;
from the bark a tiny bat came loose,
dropped dazed into a pallet of soot.
But with mouse spine pressed flat, he
laid out the absurd wings of skin,
and fledged with that only,

in time engaged the stone.

The Hopper Light

We are left out of every future except one.
This is a weakness that grows more obvious
as I turn the pages of the catalogue. How
when the light squares off, for instance,
the people will already have gone off
like bright boats into the "future perfect."
Or gotten boxed into rooms where the sun hounds
their solitude and ferrets out its yellow edge.
There light discloses the pathways and divides

where the flesh breaks down, and fragility,
like spiky winter trees, moves in.
For light here's the medium in which we are
the old, frank questions. And that's why
only such as saltboxes stick to their alibis,
only peeling barns, our shelters and shells
weathered like spry old drunks huddled before
a judge and totally indifferent to his glaring
censorious face. Funny, the church

with its compass needle jammed against the sky
is now a museum, the god having fled.
But the light keeps up the pressure on the Rooms-
for-Rent at the lower frame and on the fishermen
just out of sight whose old wrecks
and figureheads (worthless as hood ornaments,

yet drifting, Muse-like) junk up the parallels
where there must have been pews. The title
says simply, "Methodist Church, Provincetown."

From there was a future into which even Hopper
was denied, glimpsing as he worked, his own
de-creation. From the top you might look out
and see for miles to boats and plunging dolphins.
You might see how its white upward spire invents
the morning air. For which the sun, all night
shadowed, swings free of that tyranny,
shining back with a vengeance. Then blue sky,
and always the window; always those woods.

A Hanging

(after Orwell)

The earth is bright. And the water
shines this way through the air.
Gulls float the troughs like sitting ducks
and the pleasure boats sleep. Do you think
you could wag your whole body

at the sight of so many human beings together?
Like a good salt citizen I shiver
at the light's breaking and turn
to my inward work: too much
forgetfulness has made a mess of things.

Do you think a heart, falling,
shows on the circuits of a face?
I mean the way the wind stops just before dawn.
If so, then write to me and say
why we are not lost forever.

I sometimes dream that my bed
is floating out to sea; storks
like caulking guns roost on the bedposts.
If I take this dream in a moral light
it makes me wake up good.

Linda writes, "E. sends her love.
Does that sound ominous?"
A short drop, and they level you.
Then the old, age-wise doctor and the bounding
spaniel bitch, each pulls a hanged leg

to see if we are alive
or merely dead. And if dead,
we have a hard time convincing the dog.
And if alive, we must consider
our predicament all over again.

Buckley Hollow

We were never ourselves. The boys
dipping in and out of the rock pool
slippery as otters, how could they
wrap the scene around them,
the bankside trees folding
the sun out so completely?
So you turned and said they
were unimpressive, like amateurs
sliding shamefully offstage.

In your version the waterfall
rushed down in another's name.
Smart dogs tracked rats to their holes
for the purpose of interrogation.
Even the weeds shrank when
the cottonmouths ticked past.
I hardly need mention the stallions,
those swaybacked pets cropping
towards us down the valley, clouds
lying in the hammocks of their spines.

The flocks of gorse, easily
swayed, blame the point
of your hands for entering
the same river twice, perpetually.
Like the blue smoke from a rifle

when the wind tears it apart,
I blame no one. I only return
to watch the swimmers,
their small persistence in the evening,
glistening and interchangeable.
But I am forgetting the name
for those struggles they cannot admit,
flooded to the waist, their black
torsos like a breathing target.

Dead, and already the absence
is too proud to tell me something.
If seeing the angles produces
a second sight, when does it end,
the vision of missing parts,
this conspiracy of the grasses?
The need to mean the end
hovers about this randomness
the way conversation sits broken
over a bed when a dog is barking,
when innocent slivers of that
complete the summer moon.

Prisoners Bathing

Beneath the wall
they remove their clothes.
Prison issue twists off whole
like the skins that snakes
squirm out of in the woods.

Twenty, maybe thirty men
wait under a pipe that's drilled
with holes like stops on a flute.
Then, as in some pantomime,
the water and the washing.

Sunset does not change the fact
of the wall that bends a mile around
to shape all in its unbroken ring.
Their own shadows rise before
them, then the wall's shadow.

These projections are like sinking,
the limbs and torsos swallowed up,
but waving and bending as if time
were not critical to anything,
and they would be clean

even in their extremity.

Cleaning Vegetables

Sometimes the beet cries clearly
between the language of the knife
sunk in and the cool matter
of heart coaxed out.
Old skins like leaf-fall
pile in wet twists in the sink.

Maybe in sleep one hand washes the other;
otherwise too much imagining
would hold us off absurdly. For today,
cleaning the vegetables, I saw that
the small work grew large, brought
from random to a parable to waking.

And then another thing occurred to me
as I cut: the water took with it
the memories of other lives, the beards
of radishes and the black turnip
soils to a corner in the dark
where they couldn't get back.

Though it was possible to guess
the outcome of the disheveled mess
of bruised and roughened vegetable skins,
yet now the water meant clarity more
strongly than I'd imagined and made off

with those gathering flecks.

The feelings of misgiving flowed away
at once as the water and knife
made things especially clean. The potato
left its mealy skin, the lettuce became white,
the carrot gave up its fingerprint,
the avocado, its wooden heart.

Caught in Rain

The rain has the same effect
on birds. The rain which
drenched me, the unsubtle rain.

Now I watch the world
emerge from the other world
it took cover in. But

still thunder sounds
in the distance, breaking off flakes
of the sky like a priest

making his way along a bent line
of worshippers. *This is my body,*
he whispers to each in turn.

Birds are flying now,
worms gushed up from their holes,
junebugs glistening on swaying stalks

of grass. (My shriveled neighbor
hurries off in her Bug
for the weekly bedside visit

at the home of her terminal
friend somewhere.) It will be

like falling in love again

to feel the sky-chilled rain
wanting to press my shirt
into the likeness of my body

until I am the submissive one,
part bird, part worm, part of
what is without reason.

It will be like being
a cumbersome thing on the swinging
bridge of a leaf, naked

before the hurtling sky,
knowing only the present tense,
if I should go out again.

The Mountaintop

At the top of the mountain
I sit down by a rattlesnake skin
blowing like a windsock

on a stalk of dry grass
whose leaves
chirr in the bluster.

The whole mountaintop shimmers
and the eye moves beyond
to the hills' stabilities

and beyond that to the ocean,
where cloud-bands
level in even with the shoreline.

Above it, the light, dusty blue,
darkens toward the zenith
into a seemingly more acute

complexity.
Forty now, I hear
in the dry ratchetings

faint, repeated allusions
to other stories and times

briefly touching this one.

What matter? It's the climb
I'm after to the Wordsworthian
purview and the sublimity.

The flies buzz about.
I skim them off my clothes
like some old horsetail.

Quietly, it occurs to me,
with the range of hills
undulating in stillness to the edge of sight,

how naturally
and with what vigorous ease
the flies have flown to the mountaintop.

Buried Head

A bumblebee strafes the aged gold mines.
In the garden, magnificent rot: tomatoes eviscerated,
hanging like bags; sunflowers that were once
bright pies on stakes, bend and crook into canes.
In the fields, stopped wheels of hay, implying journey,
clutter before the horizon, above which
battalions of clouds roll up and forward,
implying the end of happiness, if this is what happiness

has been. I drag wood from the garden pile,
careful of the snakes who occasionally
slither into the mix. It will be a lovely
tinderbox fire, the kind one would expect
of a phoenix. Whereas in fact, these stacked
combustibles were recently the joists and structure
of an old massive wing, until a tornado
arrived one day and quickly settled their hash.

Stick by stick, I will feed the house to itself,
as I have cannibalized myself to make
the fire brighter. Up through the chimney
and into the atmosphere from which one might
spot other lights and other fires in preparation
for future engagements. Afternoon drags
through the yard like an old dog, beside which
cars flash down the highway into town.

'd with kids, my eye
ʰuried in the grass.
ᵗ the porch
s, weeds,
ᵧven up any sense
ᵤ, whose rhythm
, ᴅe it broken down
ᵤons or Sahara-wide minutes.

ᵤparrows assemble on a wire that awaits
voice to prove geography a simple joke.
(And if geography, why not time?) One darts
away over the firehouse. Tonight's freeze
will strangle the mist of gnats that floats
at the screen and supersede all this
buzzing and yellowness. Suddenly, nothing
will seem so important as getting up half-frozen
just to see the sight of that gun-metal hair.

Crickets

They are without memory, making
up the night's story continually,
like Scheherazade. They are the old men
who pull the wool caps down
over their brows after the fashion
of railway baggage clerks.
They limp, paying no mind
to a missing leg. They crawl
in the bottom of bait buckets
knowing there is no exit.
When the grass grows thick
as the pile of a Persian rug,
and intoxicated with rain,
bully with heat, they are there
picking their way through tropical
forests. Then when night comes
and with it desire, and with it
love, and with it love's decline,
and with it death and the second death,
they take their place in the orchestra.

Atomic Future

My father returns from his garden
to his chair. He is worried about me,
recalling the specter of unemployment
and the old tyranny of debt. He worries
too about his legs, bum now, the veins
long since pulled out like squash webbing.
Legs that must still propel him daily
to his dried-out bean rows and back.
To the deck, den, stairs, and thence
to bed. Like me, he has no other choice

but to make it work, whatever "it" is.
He flips open a copy of *Omni* and reads:
"Atoms will rotate around each other for
the universe's lifetime without showing wear."
Sounds that emerge this fall evening,
as if no longer toggled to bodies, spread forward:
children's shouts mix with the staccato
barking of the smaller, more paranoid dogs,
which in turn connects with the bug Muzak.
Finally, like an afterthought, a jet

somewhere moles upward through clouds,
routinely transcending the sky cover.
Perhaps he should worry. After all, I'm
those same atoms reconfigured into this self,

spinning exactly to the end of my lifetime.
But first I have to figure out the cash-
flow problem and afterward superimpose
the "what-if?" scenarios of the next
few months onto my worry screen
like the transparent overlays that build

a frog in a child's encyclopedia. I think
of him taking extra jobs, when my mother
would silently place the pot roast down
on the trivet, exhorting us, with a look, to eat.
Now retired, he delves into the structure
of atoms and stages in the lives of the galaxies,
meanwhile worrying about the stages
of my checking account. He reads on:
"They will clasp each other with the exact
same degree of force forever." The beans,

stunted and desiccated by drought,
hang like an old pianist's arthritic fingers.
All summer his tiller raised nothing
so much as golden dust. Still he stands
by the dry bed of the garden, at the white
string rectangle that outlines its promise.
He is like a madcap football coach inventing
razzle-dazzle plays to save a victory,
though the players and fans have long
since disappeared down the maw of time.

I will have to do some fancy footwork soon.
That's clear. And I know there's some further
humiliation waiting. I can sense the remote
patronizing gaze bearing down like faint
starlight from the end of the Milky Way,
arriving in time to catch my father dozing
off in his chair. It will hang like vapor fuzz
on the skylight until the zodiac drags it off.
For that, I will gradually grow a carapace,
or find more pity in the flesh—I don't know.

The evening's heavy sonic wave becomes
the night surf. Somewhere upon that relay
is a voice trying to get through to explain
about the bonds holding matter together.
I'm ready to record that message and store
it in the same memory register where
my father is arriving from the night shift.
He places his black empty lunch pail
on the table. He's been loading boxes
onto trailer trucks, and his legs are stiff.

I see his fingers wrap around the door
as he looks in on us, his face obscured
by the light behind him. Because I'm broke
I don't want that memory to have to live
by itself anymore. He scrapes together some
leftovers, perhaps spaghetti, or a pimento
cheese sandwich my mother has left out.

We hear him moving about the kitchen
for hours, postponing minute by minute
the sleep that will stop his legs for a while.

La Bohème

Someone said it was like country music.
It was clear what she meant, the way it gets
hooks into you faster than you can protect yourself.
And close to life, too, as when you peel away
the layers of interference: clothes thick and ill-
fitting, the zest with which the hero's roommates
approve the echoes of each other's banter,
while furtively observing her from the corners
of their slum. Still, it's the way it happens
there in the dark: love's expiring air, reeling
out a sumptuous music as it goes—and dawn
rising to contrast the poverty of the whole thing,
absorbing stars as the scene changes. Conveyor-
belt silhouettes glide by outside, bored
and unconcerned with the fat girl everyone's
made such a fuss about. Just like country music.
You know you should get up, make your way
following whatever threads of pride you still have left.
But you stay, letting it happen, convincing yourself
of its significance, as she, leaning up from her deathbed,
cuts loose and goes straight for the last-row hearts.
And you sit back while the endless swansong drills
your sternum as if it were a rock, against every instinct
that could have meant something more dignified,
before the death and the pity started,
before it all got so terribly out of hand.

Mozart

I had a fantasy about size,
that we were all terribly small
in the field of each other's memories.
That we were scattered and subject
to the direst revisions.

Naturally I want to be whole
again, as in childhood,
and the proper size for thinking
about. But again is a fantasy too
when you think about it.
There are no agains, only approximate
repetitions we say hello to
as if greeting acquaintances at work.
Pretty soon the trenches get rearranged,
and then where are we?

From this distance the cows are brushstrokes.
They should thank God for filing
them under the dumb animals.
After a while they become dots,
then just a smell as they graze
toward the farther pasture, just
something that passes through the nose
like dust through a screen.

My house is in reality a *gemütlich*
little rattrap, and this a rat's lyric,
the wind that only tractors ahead,
eliminating, by way of passing,
both music and the Muses.
I wish that it were a white mansion,
and that there were a man walking
through, his sweet limbs swinging
as he held the heel of a violin
against his jugular. Because
of all the notes, there must be
one somewhere resolving itself,
making its signature thrust—a wedge
into the eventual silence,
like the vanishing point in a landscape,
and that one note, like the silence,
he wouldn't play.

The Word "World" in Jarrell

If I think about it, I get lost when I see
a new slab put into place. What was yesterday
ground is now foundation, and arriving for
their constitutionals, the mockingbirds blench.
Construction cranes transform the air
into boxes of itself. Will I alone
be the unchanged one? Who am, myself,
a long box of echoes? If I don't get
the words right, the new library
rises in spite of me. This means
more explaining on my part, like a baker
who's stopped to sneeze, and the loaves
back up. Damaged, I'll nonetheless lean
to the thing that's moving beyond me.

The long waveform of the oak branches:
I used to walk by here on my way to work,
and the stylish trilling of the birds
followed exactly the predictable bird-
language of Heraclitus. Now deflected
from this square of world, their songs
struggle against the straitjacket of their
occasions, and I'm no longer sure, among
so many unsettling givens, what the debate
is still about, or that debate at all
describes what this contention really is.

Once I stood by Jarrell's grave and smelled
the boxwoods sweetening the field, the same
shrubs that had sweetened my childhood.

And I remembered that a Fragment describes
how, in Hades, souls perceive by smelling,
as the flow of past life is jarred loose
in spring. Structurally speaking,
slab and bookshelf are identical. What
melancholy, then, ravels text with the word
"word"—as if one brought the other
into being by will or some dark power.
Or book were to word as "world" is to this
shifting habitation. Instead, the birds
are dabs of pathos, and songs lean automatically
toward their shelves. Already I have to go
a new way to work, and things, I know,
are not going to be so easy as they once were.

Autobiography

As soon as you leave you enter
memory, and that small emissary
of yourself immediately loses
its credentials. No longer yours,
you can't recall it, or send it
instructions on tactical lying.
You may have armed yourself with
heavy qualifiers, been Henry James,
but turn your back, it's theirs.

Thus, memory. And each fresh
installment of yourself, though
exquisite, is still lump clay.
Even the other tack, sincerity,
has zero chance because revelations
have nothing to do with memory.
Trapped, you have only the whim
they toss at you to put on.
You are a small being now, just

a fraction of the old self.
Your mother tongue begins to suffer,
like an émigré's. Plainly, you
were the aggregate of what you gave
up. Now you are suspiciously
plural. What is happening to you?

It is like glimpsing someone who
favors you in an old movie
you used to like. And yet,

the costume is absurd, not to
mention the horse. Or these
others, also with your face, jerk-
ing their spears in the air.
Spilled change, their faces turn
briefly to the you they obviously
can't see. And the barbaric
shouts they make, this cast of
thousands swarming over the dust!

God's Tumbler

What perishes will reappear

as the clouds come
gathering our shadows
and giving them back again.

From the pool I looked out
and saw the green
launched out of the earth

behind the lying bodies.
What a green it was,
and no one, I thought,

had ever seen it so.
A helicopter flew over
and then a bird whose

mysterious purpose seemed nonetheless
apt. But the foundation of this
building where my life ripened

into today
became something else
as I looked down.

Suspended, it might well
have levitated
were it not as

dependent as anyone could make it.
I wished then that
somebody had been around

to applaud and corroborate
this Wallenda-esque, high-wire
fact of gravity

that dangled the building
before me like a splendid
joke, if only because

it seemed it could have come unhooked
and fallen, against reason
into sheer air.

The proximity of that
chaos brought you, my friend,
to mind,

and nothing moved,
as I could imagine it moving
but stayed firmly in place.

A little tumbler—

so the legend goes—
when asked to produce his offering

at the Virgin's shrine
stood directly and at length
on his head

to the amazement of
his pious colleagues who were
further astounded

by the laughing Queen
and company of Heaven
suddenly in their midst.

Even from that perspective
he must have seen both
the emptiness under his feet

and the inverted figure
of himself, which had to make do
with the merest tissue

of being when the vision
was gone.
The trembling of foundations

is any man's fear,
an undistributed middle term

that the mind seizes on

in its mania
for survival.
Meanwhile, the birds

sing out of the green,
make nests,
and do not stare at their wings.

So in the reflected world,
washed and moving
like the water itself,

I imagined you again,
who reminded me of the willing acrobat.
And you were alive for me

whom I had thought dead.
But what perishes
reappears

according to a primordial plan
whose existence I learned of
reading a book

I had opened casually
beside the water
of a swimming pool.

And was implicated
by memory and emptiness
in its simpler,

perfected longing.

Sunbathing

Something in each of these bodies
will never happen again.
And so they situate themselves
around the pool, as if the streams
of light will mean
it was finally all right to be
a secret, like the torsos of cherubs
with chunks torn out of the backs.

The older lie in a different way,
sometimes turning awkwardly on their sides
as the young would never do.
It is a posture for regret,
poising that way as if
the earth were closer, and they
carrying a burden more physical,
whereas they are actually

emptier. Lying around this
rectangle that precisely reflects
the undeviating blue, they
simulate sleep, if they are not
sleeping, and this is as true
as it gets in the sun,
a few hours of meanwhile,
the night tilting upward.

The Mermaid

Both freshly divorced,
my brother and I met at the shore
for the brief solace of a holiday.

His eyes still sparkled
as he reeled in a twisting, liver-colored
shark and, wedging it

underfoot, carefully removed
the steel hook that pierced the lip,
then kicked it back into the sea

as the pier crowd looked on.
"You can see all kinds of things
if you stay out long enough,"

he explained, "and you have
enough beer." His son romped along
the planked surface that seemed,

at night, to stretch aspiringly
over the water, whereas we recognized
its incompletion: it was just

another failed bridge.
Watching the boy, I remembered

the times his father rode

on my shoulders up ravines, through
thickets of ragweed, timothy and cinquefoil
looking for the secret places

of our myth, where no one could find us.
We knew that these places—the hollows,
the dark stands of poplar,

the blackberry brambles—
were ours to be lost in and that
no harm could come to us

there. His son would dream
that privacy too, drifting to sleep
in his pallet above the waves.

Later, fished-out, we looked in
on the island's one immemorial hangout,
a bar called The Mermaid.

Sliding into our booth we watched
the dancers bob and drift to the beery
crooning of a cowboy band.

Bathetic and wistful, but at the same time
entranced, they enacted the forward-looking
poses of love, that old addiction,

whose conclusion, later and far
out into the night, the many nights,
had always equaled, for us, defeat.

As the couples loomed by,
arms looped like block and tackle,
I asked my brother, "Would you

do the same thing over again?
I mean knowing what you know now."
My question issued from

a fictional innocence, like those places
we'd forgotten, yet managed to carry in some
remote store of memory

that now was suddenly worked
into focus with the enabling merger
of booze and song.

He looked out onto the floor
and said nothing for a long time
two or three times at least,

two or three stories, any of which
would do to swell the pedal of his own.
Then swung back around

and breaking into a smile,

said, "Of course! Wouldn't you?"
With the keeper's duty, I added

my yes, answer carrying him
to a place where all possibilities
contained every future at once,

where girls lured boys
into the blissful, rocking sea of their arms
and all distances vanished

in the zero of a mouth.
For without doubt this was our fraternity too,
to become entangled in the bright

dream of women, moth-drawn, shriveled
with a thousand hungers so that our defeat
became the sacred ground

of a future memory. And thoughts
of those cul-de-sacs now beyond reach
were not true memories at all

but empty scrub and bracketed,
bare ground, culmination of ruin's will.
What our parents knew

we took, replaced, and so failed
them, as we failed the others when, through

the intimate bridge of their looks,

we saw the pier end,
the ocean heave with fabulous fish
and we were not satisfied.

Now, we rose well before closing
and made our heavy ways to the door.
We knew what was in store,

what the dry socket of the moon,
floating in its chill bed, had made fantastic
in us. But tonight we only walked

back to the sleeping child, with the sea
grinding, the frogs exultant, and paused there
in the road to give the couples

the doubtful benefit of a smile,
the lunatic couples propped by their trucks
under the sign of The Mermaid.

Bermudas

You don't honestly think this
a retreat. The clouds
puff into cones, but your resist
the summarizing impulse which,
for others, reiterates
a sense of well-bring. Here

you are marginal. The sun finds
everything out, exposing the air
to every kind of division. There's Spain,
like longing, where the sun has been,
like the end of life, sitting at the end
of waves, or the truth

that lies at the end of deception.
The sound of a power-
saw and lumber stacking: even
in the stress of confinement
they're finding ways to elaborate
the theme of a respite.

To you it is a ratio, what a life
would be, reborn as geography.
Overhead, jumbo jets stuffed
with tourists flicker between clouds.
It doesn't matter that this

indifferent completion of bodies

jades the green body of the island.
       Beyond the golf carts,
the ocean lifts its glass shoulders.
Behind, the houses
       in their white hats lie frozen
on the hillsides. If you

    had such a house, anchored at sea,
       jutting into the massive,
mystifying figures of clouds,
would you know that you were also
       moving? That your house
belonged also to the flyaway

clouds? True, there is little comfort,
       but what it would have meant
is not, in any case, clear. These pines
prickle at the rock's edge,
       and below, the froth slips up the sand.
You are in the middle

of your life, and because there is
       no rest for the currents,
no end to the shores and limits,
it is not enough to be
       in the middle of things that
require a human's certifying gesture.

A sail's isosceles white,
        with a black "35," like the price
    snipped out of a book, tips
against the horizon.
        The sailors, though busy, wave
    at anybody. But you

    turn, enduring the reductive
        confidence of their going,
    which, with each cheerful goodbye,
throws its shadow like the net it is,
        while they shrink, yawing and listing
    in their tiny boat.

White

The computer screen glows
with the mild indifference
of a new spring day. It is my
substitute for the cerulean
that I bring forward into night.
It serves like a Death's Had
to an Enlightenment dandy.
It covers "what-is-the-case"
like Sherwin Williams.

Midnight. The crystalline
laughter from the apartment
above has become more
intermittent and threatens
to subside altogether, as if
it had surrendered to the rain,
the tapping no one turns for,
to see, at any rate, nothing
but the courtyard birdbath.

Whose dumb angel does not
prevent me from reading:
"In the wisdom of my failure,
I will carry even the last agony
to the grid of meaning."
I mean to paste these lines

to the artificial sky, to fill
its memory screen for a time,
while I sit back, as objective,

as anonymous as snow.
No longer the nosy curator
of my own dusty museum,
I have become philosophical.
Each reduction enriches me
like a quarry into which
the weather loves to come:
the snow of tradition, the rain
of knowledge, all one there.

I hear the laughter again.
Meanwhile, the cats stretch,
yawn, and make biscuits
with their paws. I think
of how love came and ended,
two storms, and yet I retained
my pronoun like a prize-
fighter his unwearable belt.
I drag this thought to the grid.

The screen, thanks to my human
snow, is becoming the brightest
light in the room. I will lend
myself to its blessed storm
until its growing white folds

into the general memory of
what was, that other storm
I sought shelter from, that rolls
like a wave through the world.

The Trawlers at Montauk

Because happiness takes a tremendous
toll, the fisherman's joy gasps
in the greasy hold, just as lovers suck
the surrounding air nearly to a vacuum.

And yet, one's life lumbers by
like a trawler, torn, top-heavy.
"Built by greed," says the ocean.
"Buoyed by hunger," say the nets.

The boats can't stay in one place.
You look again, and they've turned
to the horizon. Soon they are
almost nothing, who killed many fish.

And the sky rises alive from the ocean.
Dr. Chekhov said that men with hammers
should shadow us always, reminding us
of our unhappiness—a thought

bright with moral charm but likewise,
and finally, dark. It would require
a parallel universe, and in time they
would lay down their hammers, exhausted

and appear, hands outstretched,

mouths open, asking the same pittance
we had always taken for granted
in the soft voice, where hunger begins.

Secondary Road

Coming home in the curdling traffic
on an errand remote from my life,
turning the radio dial distractedly,
I came upon the *Liebestod*, of all things,
right where the freeway grades into my
secondary road. With that, the first sweet airs
of another summer rushed in,

which I'd forgotten. Or stretched beyond
memory of the swells of throes,
the inconsolable, world-excluding drama
of the self. Now, sealed in my car,
hurtling over the small hills and through linked,
endless fields of corn, I felt that shuddering
overtake me again

and for a few minutes the mystery of it
held on and threw me back: that lacerating thrill,
that death to reach a star . . .
But more charitably, my wonder,
as the sky darkened to evening, and I drove
through the country alone, streaked clouds above,
everywhere the thickening leaves.

Anymore

Something has suddenly ended.
Maybe the cat looks up coincidentally.
Maybe she stares her dream of the world
outward into the room, or maybe
I do.

But something is over and done with.
It's become fact, or maybe history.
Or it travels wobbling into oblivion
where it's whole at last.

The empty wine bottles have candles in them,
and someone's moved who once
ate a meal. The clock strikes three
as though it were only that,
without antecedents, and just as suddenly
it tells a different story.

Something has ended, and the air
keeps coming out of the fan.
The songs of the crickets: what were they
in my father's childhood?
What was the color blue
in his sky-blue eyes?

The river could just about take me

where I want to go, only
another would arrive and be greeted
by strangers, accept their compliments,
endure their nostalgia, and so forth.

One should wear snow shoes
so as not to fall through the world.
This is an after-song, the color blue,
and a cricket: for something has gone down
like a cat from the shelf.
And something has ended
and won't come back anymore.

Collected Poems

The telltale spoors
under the jacket-flap of this
big book, this lifework,
hint more loudly of it than
the plain printer's box of
the obituary page, the names
lying down to rest at last
within their little squares.

Slowly, nature erases culture
and life streams through the window
invisibly, in spite of gravity.
So the train's solemn double horn
gives out a double meaning
as it strains down the rusty track
under the Mississippi bridge.
I can take it, or if I can't

I don't want to be the final
mention of my attempts when I am
less spine than this.
I don't want to be the first whisper
either, of the error I will be
when I lie in memory of such
a river, replaced by spoors
drifting down from the dark waters.

Stars in Leo

Across the way, a slat-barred terrace box
juts from a glass-doored apartment
and provides the evidence of life you need:
the barbecue pit surmounting a tripod,
the canvas sling seat, nested parsons
tables on which no reading matter
accuses the trivia-bedeviled resident.
You're always surprised by the neighbors'
non-appearance: it forces the eye away
and up to the mountain ridge horizon
where the air takes leave of miles-
distant brush—the flat-bottomed
brush of a vacuum cleaner attachment
turned over—and becomes sky, endless
and scrubbed-out with cirrus interruptions.

It's fall. The summer-gummed mind,
clotted with incidents of its own slowing,
slowly quickens. "A long way" doesn't
matter now, nor a short way add much
by way of coda. The second hand creeps
up between one glance and the next,
expeditiously, like a compass
hypnotized by Platonic Forms
of northness, certitude, salvation
in coordinates that it means

to offer up on its egg-white plate.
Meanwhile rotating, phantasmagoric,
the revisionist watch apes the zodiac,
motioning the moments through intersections,
the stoplight being dead.

Night rises from the mountains,
and the grains of stars scatter the empty
backdrop. The hours honey their inhuman
runnels like water crowding through grass.
All is in the short run lost, converted,
dumped, erased but these pinholes like those
in Easter eggs, suggesting what color,
what never-to-be-realized nature
the mind might make.
Heraldic creatures rim the mountain
with only as much light as will
confound utter darkness.
The lion sleeps in his electric mane;
the neighbor's window comes on
behind the translucent skin of a shade.

The mountain is what it came to be
so long ago that no memory of it struggles
any longer in the nets of stars, no eye
lifts from its page to look down
the imagined corridor of its past:
no sight to take you through the rock.
A towel swings from the veranda

on a wire. You can barely make it out,
but its dim rectangle promises
an immaculate white, like an empty folio page
illumined by its own immensity
of reusable beginnings; or perhaps
only by sunlight—discriminate, dramatic—
far away in a future of hours,
as morning sweeps the valley.

Leaving Old Durham

I.
A one-eyed wildcat prowled the sweetgum limbs.
though the neighbors who spoke of him
have moved away or died, and he is long extinct.

I saw him once at dusk: heraldic, wary, torn,
the X's of his hears at full extension, as if fixed
to scissor the future's *néant*. The leonine shag

of his mouth made a portal such as you see
in one of the lesser Mozart operas, before which
the king, with supernatural generosity,

renounces his claim to love—in the name
of his country—and forgives his best friend
the assassination he had plotted. The head

appearing here and there among branches
was just as Roman as this sleepy *pax*.
And so it seemed: the last wildcat retiring

into the summer branches, leaving only a clack
of shuttered leaves, taking a souvenir glimpse
with the cold pupil of his remaining eye.

His flashlight scanning the yard from green
to black, from the leaves to the dark air,
my father called me in and for the first time

I had a feeling that some great shift
was underway, preceded by small, shadowy
movements too indistinct to be detected

by any but the most devoted eye, one not
left merely to time-lapse caprice, but outside,
solidly alert as the pyramid on a dollar bill,

under which a new order raises the salute.
That night of the one and only sighting,
I lay in bed, not sleeping, my whitened face

turned to the open window. Noises were
nearly visible: animals in the ordinary extremity
(or do I mean: extraordinary naturalness?)

of desires and deaths, nocturnal efflorescence,
nightly failure. And if not visible, no matter—
invisibility made a dark joy all its own.

When manic junebugs slammed the screen,
it seemed night's own carapace surging,
then retreating to democratic hollows and fields.

Here mindless, teeming tens of thousands
regrouped for the instinctive, dreamy plunge.
One night, I heard, or thought I did,

the cat's cry deep in the woods, but saw
only the red, blinking point of a water tower,
stars setting in the forest—now houses—

II.
each star pulled down "to curdle darkness,"
as Nerval put it. It is 1954. Durham simmers
in the steam of factories, steeps in the perfume

of tobacco, curing only itself, drying
to kid leather, its liquor recycled to humidity.
I wander through a field nearby with a child's

intermittent purpose. Sheep crop
the warehouse lawns, where, emerging from
their grimy nimbus, both slave and master,

semis plod past a checkpoint. The flock grazes,
floating, self-possessed, a weather front of
unconcern, somewhere coming in, moving on.

In this same grass, I reach to pull up a baby-
fat fist of clover; pull back instead a blazing welt
and through sheets of tears spy the bee-

perpetrator disappearing into heaven. What
my mother must have seen was a look
of incredulity, not of pain, or only of pain

at the aborted gift. And felt, too, a brute
courage, like the obdurate sheep when
bull-snorting tractors menaced the gate.

My dad and his pals surge from the factory
mouth at the lunch whistle, where we wait,
I in suit and cap, my mother bracing her purse

against her patent leather belt. Like a prince,
I own the hour in my ego's nutshell.
Such post-war composure—the chary victor's

evening shadow—already fogs the decade,
in whose time's arithmetic, no subtraction
or division yet make their operators known.

We cross the hot tracks between buildings
with filmy, industrial windows, stroll out
to a hole-in-the-wall named "Amos 'n' Andy's,"

whose door-centered logo melts into
a dramatic, shadowed crescent, tapered
but unambiguous. We squeeze into school

desks posing as seats, Mother in navy, Daddy
in khaki, and ceremonially unwrap the hot-dogs.
Plant workers crowd by: a pastoral pool

table beckons through the door in back,
where I'm not allowed. Daddy jokes our dogs
haven't achieved perfection until slathered

in the cook's forearm sweat. Mother turns
at this, folds her napkin and watches passersby
who cross and recross behind the reversed,

III.
painted letters. Many are black (the passersby).
My father explains that they live in Hayti
(pronounced Hay-tie), south of the tracks, where

periodically spilled like shelled peas from
the Southern Crescent, they were too weary to push
on to D. C. The story is variously embroidered

but ultimately unknowable in the dissonant
logic of smoking slums, chattering in winter,
charred in summer, cowled in meanness.

A negative standard to whites (not that
any we knew had spent time there),
They say, "What? Are you from Hayti?"

DAVID RIGSBEE   101

They call it, without irony, a hotbed.
Here, James Brown would come after the show,
seigniorial priapic, elusive. Papers have

a field day with the allegations and suits.
Meanwhile, a shopping center rears from a lot.
Main Street braces for the slow inversion

as vectors realign. But some stores
will wait out the shift, make adjustments.
Soon they will be infamous as footnotes:

Woolworth and Kress forced to trial,
for this is history; it is also a state of affairs.
The lunchroom counters become plaques,

their shame wiped clean, become what they
are now: a sift of memory, a reverse radiance,
a shadow beckoning at the edge of the yard.

Like its namesake, sooner or later Hayti warms
to its real theme, of which it is its own symbol,
separate, fiery as a love-note. But now,

heads are left uncracked; they float by
our comedy restaurant like birthday balloons.
We unwrap the remaining dogs; the aroma

of chili escapes, followed by mustard
and an acrid burst of onion. Amos leans against
his cab, distracted. Andy fancies a new suit

and bowler in the shop window, while Sapphire
unloads on the Kingfish, unmans him over some
infraction too late to fix because it is too late.

We walk my father back to work, take the bus
to our side of town, past legions of blackberry
bushes and trees sagging with honeysuckle.

Like the poet at seven, my mind slogs
through its savannas and seven seas, finding
adventures unmoved by issues, heroism

IV.
without overhead. In the city I have lost,
the dead luxuriate. Now the bourgeoisie
of a necropolis, they no longer turn in tender

stupefaction to see earth movers scrape up
the last bucolic pools of green. They prefer
the permanence of their present quarters.

Miss Riley is dead, whose pronged feet and cane
hobbled to church like a secretary bird, and Miss Tilley,
the Latin teacher, who boasted that, thanks to her,

thousands remembered the correct way to say *agricola*.
And my grandmother—all the top-heavy ladies
of the South in books. Mr. Hall, our pint-sized

principal is dead, whose cruised the school
with a ping-pong paddle, and the Bullocks
who harrowed the last farm in the neighborhood.

And not to forget Freddy—something—
the little hood who ruled our schoolyard:
shot dead. Whom the Wall remembers.

And Buck, friend of my father's youth,
whose lungs his life devoured. Did they know
their leaving was already prepared for?

Did they hear the tumblers falling into place?
did they tussle first with free will and then
necessity in that sequence that squeezes

the brakeman's pupils to a rat's glare?
Or did the subtle slippage spare them
everything but the looming intimations,

for which ceremonies were contrived where
the anxious sense could enact its anxiety?
Forty years later, self-sentenced, my parents

exiled themselves, but they bore the town
on their backs, complete with its heat, contention,
its death, like history inscribed on the backs

of turtles reassured by the horizon's immobility.
It's summer solstice when I look up, and I want
to amass more images, without knowing which

or how they have been hiding all these years.
Nor to what purpose, except to witness how
these dead live to vex each other's shadows.

The ancient, deciduous trees have thinned out.
I remember how they once soared into tent poles
that we wandered among , looking for the show.

But I don't know what became of the cries that issued
from their branches, or of the brilliant, watchful eye
that was, was said to be, and so drifted into legend.

Four Last Songs

After Strauss, *Vier Letzte Lieder*
in memory of my brother (1954-1992), a suicide

1.   *Spring*

IN HOLLOWS GOING TO DUSK/I DREAMED A LONG TIME

Once more I got up and put on the CDs;
once more, hunched in a blanket, I remembered
        the gold-grieved crickets
had disbanded, retired to the silence.
                I wanted this music
                        to iron back the hush of that,
                of the possum, whose cracked smile
                        and fetal comma,
sick of foraging, punctuated the hollow of a log;
                of the nesting squirrel I rescued—by depressing
                my foot—from fatal indecision
                        in the zigzag alley of the street.

                I wanted to make room
for the street lamp bestowing its refrigerated light
                        over the quiet neighborhood,
                for the nacreous reading lamp smeared
                        over the nightingale spines,
                upright, but sleeping among the bookcases,

row on row—impossible—
where even the word *and* abutted
a slope of silence.

I shivered meanwhile,
wondering how the lack of sleep would connect
with your sleep. Sitting upright, I never-
theless desired to go under and closed my eyes
to let the drift come on.

Since he is silent, do not lose this chance . . .

I heard Schwarzkopf warble the first bars:
a long time—where the phrase ends—
is the high note, and long, a keening
that arrives so very quickly
that one is surprised
she's onto the subject already,
having dispensed with the little,
indistinct preliminaries.
Perhaps it was because
there is an upward drift—a slope—to histories,
which are thoughts redressed,
going to the engagement in the expectation
that afterwords will have scaled
and peaked, will have said the most
to the uncertainty of fresh air.

Jessye Norman caresses

the height, handing it over to darkness
and maternal warmth, "the sound of water
weeping in the Bernini fount,"
but unexpectedly,
since we look back at the simplicity

OF SPRING TREES, BLUE SKIES, FRAGRANCE AND BIRDSONG

from isolated heights,
whose vantage makes even the nearest days
and plainest words ambiguous.

It is a long way back. *It is a long way back*
and in need of warmth.

Parmenides held the One
to be inviolable,
the paradise of integers, if we but submitted
life to reflection. But in my
reflection, I saw also your snail's slick
paved toward the trees,
and I hailed you in the spirit
of that separation
(this is the voice print of that separation),
that going with and without,
that speech

now spreading into a hollow
uniformly available to the human noise.

There were hollows where we went,
　　spring-born, spring-loaded,
already trailed by flashlights and cries
　　a long way back: what more?

Another light penetrates the hollow-
ness that admits separation and moreover defines
　　　　　　　　it.
　　　In spite of which we dreamed
of woods, dreaming ahead, where we were not,
　　　　　which is to say
　　we came into our own, but
　　　　　　　but
　　　　with divergence,
　　fecundity, difference, sex, inspiration,
　warmth, otherness, recognition, music.

　　For you, everything took place
on the plane of the body, and you therefore
　　joined, effortlessly, the dead,
　　　　　　　but speak . . .

　　　　　How it felt
　　was its meaning.
　　　　Even your note
drew the police's attention to aesthetics—
　　　　drawing inferences from "style,"
　gripping the page sideways, holding it flat

against the light—as if

one of the last songs wouldn't also be the twitter
of remembered birds,
(a twitter that flutes up
at the end, where art loosens
and passes into nature).

NOW YOU STAND REVEALED
as if you had become a message swaddled in quotes,
something *about which*—like
a remembered spring.

But even as remembered
you stand whole, an accomplishment
(of desire, perhaps), of which

I send forward the virtual echo
from my own escarpment.

Were the springs therefore rich and resonant? Or
do I file the official report merely stating
in plain words
that summer destroyed
with exaggerated speed and fall followed suit
(the season you prophetically liked best
because-ahead of schedule-it previewed death
wistfully, as romance)?

It was like trying to read an embryo's green lips.
I tried to remember spring. And now music's (dis)consolation,
                    creating a backwave to memory, its wind
                              gathering the green up
                                        and letting it down again
          (*es zittert durch all meine Glieder*, in the words
          of Hesse = you, deaf, moved by the same)

and so I tried to read . . . because to read spring
                    was to read the other,
          was to address the other who stood

          SHINING IN THE FLASH FLOOD OF LIGHT

          that poured into the sockets, the hollows,
                    the cranium prepared, if necessary,
          to amplify the light, to sink its own hole
                              to tunnel out the other side,
                                        if necessary,
                    trailed by flashlights and calls on the two-way,
                    the house sacked by police
                                        where

          YOU RECOGNIZE ME, CALL TO ME
              AND MY BODY SHAKES

          because this is not the last song;
                    death, but not even

                              the last song; rather

in the manner of this racket to your skull
that I translate into music

but speak . .
and then such sweetness suffusing the empty hall.

2.   *September*

Like the palm at the end of Stevens' mind,
it stood,
like a rose gibbeted on the end of its stem,
like a cigarette at the end of an arm,
that last thought that one previewed,
that one was about to think
with the head
that stands on the end of the neck.

Here it is September, where weariness is previewed
in abundance, where desultory fires
flicker and subside.
Wind catches the smoke
and bears it aloft like a ball of raving gnats
or the vapors of a prayer.

But THE GARDEN SENSES

cool rain. Out there, I'm almost beginning to remember
it
clearly, the symbol of my affection.

Is he signified in a flower's exhausting push?
He, at least, showed
enough dissatisfaction actually
to die
when flowers—substitutes—were past:
he knew they didn't correspond. And in that sense he was always
away: the eye saw and passed on. How many streets
forking and proliferating

lay in the way of
the end of his mind?

THE RAIN IS COOLER THAN THE FLOWERS

as when I spy a bumblebee,
and witness his head clubbed by a water drop,
I can feel the wings buckle
momentarily

before he rights himself, mid-air,
and adopts a parting attitude of feigned coolness.

No Edwardian twilights cushion the blow

SUMMER GOES ON TO THE END OF SUMMER

and it is astonished to find it is actually feeble
(item: "actually" = no interpretive force)

among the roses.

It is as if a drunk
turned to another drunk
in a befuddled ecstasy
and asserted: "That was no ordinary rose,

it was the goddamned Mystical Rose!"
But mostly it was falling apart,
without significance, and I happened
to remember the ends of summers with their
self-dismembering, mystical roses that said, insignificantly,

See, we will make you little believers:
reds and melon-yellows,
primaries, farewell!
We lie, burnished, expecting hell!

It noted the crossroads already
strewn with petals and leaves

for you were crossed, and in your vexation
they danced on their points and skittered about,
and spun on their toes

and lay flat, petal and petal,

LEAF AFTER LEAF, representing and yet misrepresenting you,

doing everything that can be done around a body.

(Adam had a dream, which God clubbed
from his brain

using the fist of His angel.)

Your crossed arms signify a final vexation—ironically,
in the land of the dead
the sign for peace.

SUMMER WOULD HANG FOR A LONG WHILE,

the rain would get even
cooler, the garden would close its eyes.

(As I closed my eyes, so tears emerged and fell from them.)

September. I sat staring at the dying garden,

and when I could

watch no longer, when my eyes failed me,
I considered

the road crossing and recrossing in my hands.

3. *Going to Sleep*

DAY THAT TIRES ME-
the gleam off snow,
eraser made solely of sweeping
light. Everyone trekked across snow
that day to work, and worked even

that day, as though in the expectation of a desire

to be fulfilled

in the consummation
of a starry night.
You
thought the night would receive you
MORE KINDLY, LIKE A TIRED CHILD,
(more kindly? than?); on the contrary
your own desire—even that day—

MY ABSURD DESIRE!

Now only a howling, like winter wind
around square foundations,
around bases of strange trees, escapes
into the woods,

where it becomes one with the nocturnal rumor,
a wind TO RECEIVE
time

MORE KINDLY.

Even by two, it was late in the day,
the note scribbled in haste,
the phone messages checked, the cockatiel
covered, in kindly fashion, the papers checked,
policies read in a darkening blur,
codicils, exceptions, business even now somehow
the business of life
and then
no longer your business to settle such accounts
except as the desire to do so,
to receive more kindly the elapsed hope extended others

if such is hope; frost pressed to the window
outside,

the procession of cars, everything
to do, even in the face of it,
climbing stairs at last,
everything to do, climbing the last steps
LIKE A TIRED CHILD, four o'clock
and night most definitely coming, THE STARRY NIGHT,
us.
I saw it, too, and hooded my eyes, walking
to the car, implausibly twinned, to be
doing that with only the sound
of wind
and cars beneath constellations

brightening into place

that have no sound. I saw them rising in the window
behind the telephone, and I knew
that if I stepped outside, as I was to do more than once,
and stood among the sticks, shriveled vines
and bare, heatless trunks

they would be, as the suddenly dead
of long past, abruptly summoned, on the line,
given pause, blinking as if in surprise
to find such a simple call-back

at the end of such distant footsteps.

I TOLD MY HANDS REACHING, TO QUIT,
MY MIND TO GO BLANK,
for otherwise,

thought would rush in, dispensing
its metaphorical light, and draw me back to life
and the pulse of conversation,
the business
when

I YEARNED ONLY TO FALL
AND SLEEP
AS IF MY SOUL WOULD GO UP
riding a bullet,

with a bullet's urgency,

but never falling back to earth
and its business

but only live where no life was

PROFOUNDLY, VARIOUSLY as the oncoming snow
mixed on the coming wind.

4.   *Evening Glow*

Trigger. Like a poem, you do it yourself
or you don't do it. And it travels
because you do it:

it has somewhere to go and the fact that it carries

you with it any distance is incidental:
so many feet per sec. It is the matter, to which
the creating mind can't
keep up, but only follow, streaming
through the keyhole only to find a wall, which,
in any case, it wanted,
needed, life
not being walls enough.
THROUGH SORROW AND JOY
you raised the piece, cocked

it,

stars watching at the north window,
by now we as brothers were damned, though

WE HAVE WALKED HAND IN HAND

not realizing the urgency now at the end,
not with any certainty,

for the song dips and returns, suggesting
even at the end of song we are locked
into minute particulars
of your imagined longing
and my certain regret,
pulses inside of which: yet smaller pulses,
but something to exert a pull back
from the moment, as though

only violence could bring a close

by bringing utter destruction, inadmissible
annihilation, as though the meaning of the poem also
were a torch to destruction, forcing it toward an admission:

LET US REST NOW FROM WANDERING
IN THIS QUIET COUNTRY,

sung in pressured tongues of flame,

as the mind, its webs and locked rooms
spewed forth, torn by the physical harrowing.

MOUNTAINS SLOPE ALL AROUND US,
no way to avoid coming off them,
no way to avoid the gravity, the animals
huddled in the hollows as headlights seek
their own passage

in some design you can never know, nevertheless
there
in the site of terror,

while THE SKY ALREADY DARKENS
around the figures of TWO CLIMBING LARKS
DREAMING, or
seeming in their incongruity
to dream the private narrative of themselves.

LET THEM,
I say. Let us already separate from this life,
the only life, agree to separate
from these selves, the only ones,

SO EASILY LOST, SO STUPIDLY LONELY, unaware
of TIME, insanely accelerated already,
as if howling *I am time*,
the Arcadian whirlwind
spinning your wits apart, having done as

soon as said,
the torso falling backward
FOR IT IS ALREADY TIME TO SLEEP;

the bullet at light-speed already asleep
under the dead weight, two masses, the little
and the big becoming one
so fast
that one scarcely has time to think
of the escape of thinking, except merely in terms of
an honorary thought, a presentiment:

LET US NOT LOSE OUR WAY
IN THIS LONELINESS.

By the time the sun
had found its place beneath earth,
the claret lamps of departing cars
interspersed with swiveling, too-late alarms,
the world of business emerging to meet the night,
the tramp and thud of that business
that added to the glow,
your body
was the invitation:
COME NEARER, THIS IS PEACE
this caress of the beginning of nothing
that follows after, which seems now only
momentarily interrupted by the nothing
before. Ah it is PROFOUND, as some evenings encircle

us, benignly, seriously
in the glow that stands at the end of our weariness.
Ah!

HOW WEARY WE ARE, how drawn to the silence,
enticed,
come nearer, although it is hard
to stop the wandering, the even-now curdling
narrative . . .
Having dreamed a long time, it is time to wake,
led from the present
to the distant, but
let us not lose our way
but move along the wall of silence

and cling, as he has done, to the wall of silence.

The Garden of Catherine Blake

Cloud and earth converge like banners of geese,
both undulant, assimilable
each to the other.
Though I draw the horizon line
with the eye's rule, without
question, they pass into each other.

Easter again, and this sod
with its sticks and rubbish,
its whirled grasses, as if a mower demon
had whetted his scythe to reveal our grave,
is even more of paradise than when
God rose
from the cave of the brain
and leapt to tongue like a petrel
astounding the grave academics!

I do not doubt the light behind the trees
secures a meaning and fastens it
to our despair. Or that the same slant light
skimming across the boards
where we talked the winter warm,
fanned by the wings of seraphs,
is all the unendurable fullness
of this sweet paradise.

From which, so suddenly, we rise
and join the air, exalting the matter
spread below in its circular struggle,
that was our home awhile.

Only Heaven

A rabbit turns the aerial of his ears.
He? The grass lays back, plowed
with the approach of . . .
One doesn't know what the approach is of.
His empty wit.

It is a postmodern evening in America.
It is after a lot of things. Now,
the woman cracks the door to make sure
it's him. Only the flesh of summer leaves
blocks the mystery of starlight.

Only a bicycle goes by as he slips
into the lighted crack.
The sound of the chain is seemingly amplified
as it goes from the teeth of the flywheel
to the little teeth
and out again until the sound is lost.

Until the sound is found
again, heightened, the way lovers in an opera
pass the climactic moment to strings
and lapse replaced, knowing the meaning
will be handled properly, as the last
wisps of sound disperse
into the space they used to think

the only heaven.

The Metaphysical Painters

What if, after the tulips' slow ecstasy,
the void? I see
through Magellanic clouds of veronica,
the amnesiac blankets of dandelions,
how the dark possibility
takes the lawn.

Only yesterday, last week—can't
put my finger on it—there was
a house, its eyes our eyes,
and we were in our houses traveling.
To shovel the past forward
gets us to snow's empery,
and the green swells, in turn,
to meet it.

Therefore, I
can't tell you of the provenance
of summer. The waves slaughter
themselves in rows, the ditch struggles.
They go down because it's nothing,
not the way I would take your shaping hand,
never to take up again
the mating of beauty to cruelty.

Almost You

I look through the glass and think:
how many lives does this make?
There are the deck chairs, and, yes,
that's a palm—I knew them once—
and a pool that doubles and bathes,
bathes and doubles. Until I too
am double and more, memory
a prism lighting some square-
a small pane of light, surely, but a light.

I'm getting tough and humble.
Isn't this what years are for?
Perhaps I've got it all wrong,
but I don't think so. Uncannily,
I see you now, your shattered flesh
grown transparent, and I wonder,
why have you come when I
have only this barrier to offer,
this glass and this square?

Maybe the past will speak to us,
but we won't speak to the past
any more than a fly on a window
would be, to the window, any more
than a speck. Tough and humble
is what happens: more barriers,

more scraping away, more self-
effacing until the glass is clean.
And no one looks through.

Grayscale

This is the afterlife, that I can say this
while ivy climbs down out of its pot,
and paperwhites, stem-tipped
with pot-scrubber-sponge blossoms
shoot out a stiff, astringent smell
as attention-getting as a hiss. No
explanation lurks behind the odor
to contain its strangeness; no expression
of mine can do more than tell you

of its failures. But how happy the cat
seems, yawning through the plants
transplanted to the apartment world.
Their gray shadows rise and move,
seem sometimes 3-D. Above them,
there's the unmoving shadow of a fence
in a painting, the fence going
to the vanishing point, an empty house,
sentimental, situated on a hill.

There's a scene at every window, too,
and you're not in them, but rather
generalized by this shadow that comes,
courtesy of traffic, and like traffic
leaves, only managing to distinguish
itself momentarily from the ceiling's

unceremonial blank: the insubstantial
anytime, becoming the air of paperwhites,
painted clouds over a painted fence.

But never superior to actual ones
before which winter trees become
skeletal, clapboard houses a few degrees
whiter than anyone had reckoned—
their windows and roofs, by contrast, life-
containing rectangles and parallelograms,
their chimneys channels of access
to an ineffable sky, where you might have
crossed momentarily, the color of smoke.

The Dissolving Island

No signs or proclamations
preceded the melting of the beaches.
    You went by way of touch. You
were given to think how gravity
    misshaped the bodies you encountered.

    Clouds skimmed the optic nerve.
The lean shadows of water-striders
    marbled the submerged, sunlit
columns whose ruin rose
    to the querying snouts of fish.

    A litter of shells. Your feet
fit perfectly among them,
    much better than any shoe,
and everywhere the bivalve suck,
    sand's volcanic bubbles.

    You were returning, or, it
seemed a return, for hardly had
    the descriptions arrived when
frogs hopped into the darkness
    croaking of the profit

    that comes of adventure.
Their choir turned gross, inarticulate.

The wet precincts gobbled up
their expressions, as if greetings
　　converged with farewells.

　　When the announcement came
to evacuate, the thought grazed you that
　　your feeling about starlight had been,
after all, fantasy, not fit to be thought
　　the thing it really was, the everyday-less-

　　brilliant fires, scrolling backwards,
discounting the dark, dissolving shores,
　　declining to chart how it came to be
that the figure and ground changed places,
　　that the island slid back to the sea.

Sketches of Spain

Times were better once,
before I read Spinoza
and felt his logic shake
my senses. It was like
a summons to a man
on his over-stuffed couch:
"Your reading this
indicates your compliance."

I used to clamber to the top
of a hill with my notebook
and watch what the clouds
do over the Pacific coast.
Sometimes I would take
a tape, say, *Sketches of Spain*
or some string quartet
to heighten the effect.

And here would come
a breeze bearing the scent
of Italy or Jamaica—
someplace. The thought
took me away and braced
me to walk home by
snakeskins that bannered
the dry skittering grasses.

It was just escapism,
like browsing the plates
in an art book: Poussin's
"Inspiration," for example,
where "a recumbent poet
unifies everything in soft glazes."
Before the snakes summon
him to the mountain.

But why not escape?
I keep returning for fresh
infusions, remembering,
in every renewable summer
how paradise was air; surely
the music of it was air too,
blossoming from coils
of chlorophyll and brass.

But Spinoza told me
it would be like this,
the best days assembled
in the mind, intellectual
integuments gathering
nerve, for the glaze that
paints the best days black.
That won't come back.

Spaghetti

I had not remembered, but do now.
I'm near the place: the tracks remind me
and the Amtrak horn that precedes
the escaping windows filled with no silhouettes.
It was my last Carolina summer
(money would lure me north)
that I heard the story. It concerned
a mill town early in the century
where a European circus, apropos
of nothing, like all circuses, had turned up.
Imagine how it ignited the margins of town,
not to mention the jaws of the Presbyterians,
whose profiles filled the upper windows.
Farmers looked up from their traces
and saw something extraordinary—
Hannibal's army stopping in the plains.
In this circus was an Italian violinist
who doubled as a hand: two hands
and a spine to hoist the tent, where
circus animals, too ancient for desertion,
doddered to their platforms and roared gamely,
where a ballerina danced on the back
of a treadmill palomino. One night
someone, never caught, shoved a tent-stake
through the violinist's heart. Legend
says a fight over a girl, but who's to know?

The circus vanished like foxfire, leaving
only droppings, the corpse, and some rope.
The coroner confirmed the murder,
and a judge scrawled out a writ.
But here the story gets really interesting.
Shipped to the mortuary, the corpse
was duly embalmed, but unclaimed.
The director, protesting that he
was not in the *pro bono* business,
flatly refused the burial expense.
So the corpse was suffered to wait,
in the manner of corpses, for an act
of charity he was in no position to claim,
though he could be said, posthumously,
to have desired it. Instead, he was removed
in stages to remoter rooms and finally
the attic, where, dried and tanned
as an old billfold, having lost seemingly
his dead weight, he was wired and hung
in a window. Here, he resumed performing,
but this time as a storefront crucifix, taking
upon himself the social lapses of the town.
Framed, the eye-slits and dry mouth
grimaced at the Southern depot platform.
As cracks widen inevitably to chaos, he
acquired a nickname: "Spaghetti." Railway men
and townspeople lined up to have
their pictures taken in the thief positions
by the brown monkey whose loincloth,

flanked by overalls, only hinted at the real
crux of his death, for it bears repeating
that this was the South, where,
from the symbiotic entanglements of debt
and debtor, remembrances and dis-
memberments, you must draw your own
conclusions. Everyone breathed
a complicit air, but at their own expense:
the unburied taking in the laundry
of the never-known, for instance,
if not vice versa. For air,
the great commodity, was all there
would ever be to a story like this.
But the airs of Verdi and Puccini: never
room for them, even after Europe had
given up the importance of self.
The cadaver hung in its window
for sixty years, like luck, maybe, or a warning
that we are what we are to others, not
ourselves, hard as the thought is to swallow.
Easier to murder and be damned.

Safe Box

Fresh from contemplating his own death,
now that the cancer, like rain on a carpet,
had upgraded its stain,
my father showed me the gun
my brother used to kill himself.
"Who gave him this thing?" I asked.
"I gave it to him," he said.
"Wish I hadn't done that,"
he added, as he moved to the next item
buried in the safe box.
How could it matter if, with
the defeat of language, he gave it that
smile of sweet patronage
before turning the shell of his torso,
like a drawing,
away from the succeeding view?

Hosanna

When I turned the corner,
there was something in the road,
its edge flapping like a bag.
A patrol car went by, and I
looked furtively in the rearview,
thinking of the broken headlight
I'd neglected to replace.
But there was enough light.
The possum's spine was broken,
the two halves of its body
working against each other,
clambering for either curb,
getting nowhere. I could hardly
believe my eyes: the gray
pie-slice of its head poised
on the asphalt, its paws rowing
air as if to warn travelers
of an accident, some other
scene of carnage up ahead.
As I drove by, I looked
into the imageless coins of its eyes,
and knew I would turn the corner,
in spite of thickening traffic,
in order to make an end of it.
On my first pass, a thump,
log-like, but I went around again.

I needed to make sure, and there
it was, one paw still waving.
I couldn't get my bearings:
the car missed. And missed
on the next pass, too, as I tried
to line him up where the dead
headlight was. I sickened
at my stupidity and the traffic
suddenly clotting each intersection
as I made the square back.
I knew I must aim for the head,
still facing the oncoming lane.
I switched to high beams, and
the light shot out. He was attempting
to go fetal, but the recalcitrant
spine prevented the lower half
of his body from accomplishing
this. In my vanity of wishes
I spoke to him, asking his
permission just as the left tires
made a double thump, and I knew
there was no point looking back.
Only in the aftermath of failure
can I tell you with what crooked
care I would take my own obliquities
into my hands and smooth them
like a snake straightened into
a cane, the cane compensating
for the grade of the mountain.

Only now can I imagine a word
like *hosanna*, when self-
consciousness escorts
my hulk like a slick,
when sleep is far and bound
for woods—the sticks criss-crossed
in smoky light—for the secret
paths through the underbrush.

A Dawn

As in "Nestus Gurley," the slap
of paper on wall announces
the *Globe*'s wobbly spiral,
the throw's replay connecting
with the jerky, departing silhouette
of the star-child riding his bike
farther into the suburban grid.

The man turns, one foot connects
with the rug, then the torso
asserts its general perpendicular.
As out-of-it as a Depression thug,
he stands before the mirror's
arraignment, which accepts
his image's *nolo contendere*

and offers, from behind its
neutral façade, the special razor
reserved for lifers, monitoring
the condemned's ablutions
as mournfully as a video.
Then the uniform, containing
him, as he emerges and treads

across the grass to the car.
Such drollery in the stars'

departure, such confidence
in the solar right ascension!
The drill of his mother's bones
patterns his steps into a tolerable
destiny, filling his indistinct

envelope with the little gifts
of a rote life, and his father emerges
at the end of a common day
in eternity, and sets down the brown
lunch-bag, triumphantly empty.
But first he must fold the *Globe*
under his arm—good son that he is

up to and including the retinal
surface, where the world impinges
and locks its funhouse image
in the bright reflection of his look,
then carry the frog-pond multiplicity
of worlds into his own, effortlessly,
not letting go, nor letting on.

Heat

Summer. An ochre light came
from the underside of a storm. Leaves
turned up submissively and shivered.
I saw a plane take off, turn into a crack
in the clouds. Then the crack closed over.
I sat, sweated from my damp scalp,
a secret sweat like condensation on the glass
of a judge who's fallen asleep over a stack
of motions. Lightning jabbed
its emphasis in the vicinity of the water
tower. The river like an arm in a sleeve,
pursued its out-of-body opening.

I saw under the green canopy of vines
the exact sag of the comptroller's jaws
signing his memo on budget cuts, the set
of the Inquisitors when they went to meet
the Cathars at Montségur, comfortless,
without shade. The clouds saw to that:
they willed it so, leaving only the seething
of insects stapled to their rafts of tree bark,
the hot bluster of wind from the lungs
of the coming storm. Sweating like a man
about to be corrected, I considered the rust
blistering the top of the iron tubing

that once supported a clothesline,
likewise the lost clothes hanging in waves,
whose semaphores could have spelled
an unconscious but sweeping critique
of the deepening green, the vanishing blue.
And so on, to beasts of the grass, creaking
with armor, yet programmed for oblivion,
or slinking furtively in their xenophobia,
mindlessness being a plus in any jungle.
Then manic thunder, crazier than Scriabin,
then furious rain for minutes, followed by
waltzing miasmal wisps. Growing legs,

the steam firmed up into figures bound
only to decompress into infinity.
From my hothouse, I watched, as the pageant
swiveled and bobbed, tethered to nothing,
faceless, yet something like persons.
Here, memory grew delicate and faceless
as bugs, who improved upon people
by hoisting the shields of their skeletons
against grass and stars alike. I sat still
in my flesh, and this flesh reminded me
how it would again translate itself,
faithfully, into another original.

The Exploding Man

A man explodes, showering
walls and floor with himself.
He explodes like an action-painting
in black and red. Even in
the horror of it—the slashes
and looping florets—it is not
unbeautiful. He wishes to be,
in dying, a better artist than death,
to surprise the surprising moment
and twist a blessing from its claw.

Consider how it could have been
otherwise: stoic leave-takings,
moribund whispers, loved ones
metamorphosing into mourners,
the prophetic gray matter overhearing,
"It was just as if he'd left the room,"
as they refold the Afghan over
the emaciated knees. Drooping
in his chaise he would have suffered
a fate worse than life.

Instead, the banshee trucks pull up,
boots stampede through the house.
A radio squawks the vitals'
slipping measurements to Central

as needles shove in, the mask
clamped over the nose: body
reduced to math—but body enough,
and soon the numbers grow.
The exploding man is regrouped:
a Medevac plucks his mass away.

For rescue waits at the window,
monitoring flashpoints from
the Ready position, Argus-eyed.
And of all the things perspective
can squeeze, there is this to add:
the exploding man packed into
the squares of a poem, and the poem
folded secretly into his dream, carefully
as you may imagine, being a dream.
A merely sick man opens his eyes

later, sees the puzzling bedside faces.
Beyond, low hieroglyphic clouds
melt and redraw themselves.
Nowhere are the stricken reds
and blacks. Only avatars of green.
Now he must be penitently well,
now rejoice at the stacked, knotted bags
that contain his havoc for maggots
and flies—bags of death cinched up,
dragged off by their strangled necks.

Linking Light

Nine months after your suicide,
distracted, I look up from a book
to see the picture window
draw an elemental picture.
A child fills a bucket from the blue
baby's pool and empties it again
with unthinking repetition
into the same pool.
Behind him rises the dark green of woods
where sunlight draws up and stops.
I think: even the image of you is eroding
faster than I can put it away.
The child rises, and for a moment
looks in the direction of my house,
the same moment at which
the setting sun takes brief aim
and its final light strikes his head.

Realm of Day

(La Capella San Brizio)

Some were escaping the grave,
some were standing around engaged
in the chit-chat of the totally nude,
their buttocks all balled muscle, legs
as taut as grasshoppers' springs but
calmed back into their unsurprising
place above ground. Even those
still skeletons for whom the trumpeting
angels were most exacting labor,
smiled beyond the skull's grimace.

Everything else was less surpassing—
the glory of Christ a gaslit jet
torching similar, but derivative halos.
Here and there Signorelli turned up
moments of indifferent cruelty: Romans
night-sticking poor wretches, for instance.
Even his signature self-portrait reveals
not only Fra Angelico, his friend *al fresco,*
but the struggle of a man mugged and choked
at the unconcerned artists' feet.

Then a pack of German tourists
separated us, as their guide moved

to expound the False Messiah. Their faces
managed an unnerving sameness turning to
the Last Judgment, where devils, like secret
police, joined crowds milling about a piazza
to abduct both tradesmen and their wives.
The rapt spectacles and camera lenses
sheeted to an single, tilted pane such as
the sun flares in evening windows.

At which point I drew my hand
to my face and discovered there
the morning's morning sex unwashed
enough to enter a Duomo, like the ardor
of those bodies, for whom spirit and flesh
were never wholly distinguished,
except to instruct the sight-impaired,
for whom dark was history's likeness,
and God's painted head: a flashlight
jabbing the smoke and rubble.

Sonnet

Great banks of windows only brought
suit-gray of winter green closer, canted
trunks and painterly bark, scales of ivy
under nude limbs whose colors qualified
as silhouette whether sky were slate
or no. Every so often thought-like breezes
would pass, stirring out-of-reach greenery
and palmy ferns. Then all was still again,
trees tall and empty—tall because empty
in the A-framed window (not all transparency
pointed to heaven). Here, some offered alternate
accounts of how darkness took up with glass,
how dead ones could be buried in our talk,
that silence might leave us otherwise moved.

Dream Oration

Asked to give the funeral oration for my father,
I discover I have no shirt and the ceremony
is in ten minutes. Forget the shirt. I focus
on a narrative thread that will stitch three parts
into a whole for, it seems, the benefit of my students
just now arriving from their farms, filling the athletic
arena with the wary families I observed as a child,
arranged like movie tableaux on their rotting porches.
Mounting the stage, clutching to my chest the few
sheets I haven't time to write, I adjust the microphone
and peer out onto darkened rows, feeling behind me
the doctors fanning themselves in their stifling regalia.
"The crickets," I begin, "played their quartet
in better days and minds. And when death contested
their songs, they regrouped and lived the winter
basking in the glow of a furnace, anonymously tended."
I put down the white pages and leave the hall, snatching
my shirt, fleece-like, from a hook at the entrance.
and departing down a towpath, trailed by horseflies,
passing the cemetery where new stones are being
mortared into place. Two workmen wave trowels
and I recognize the taller one as a schoolmate.
In fact, I see that I am headed for the schoolhouse,
site of honor for my father, for whose three tenses
I set the healing metronome and learned to dress
history in figures—as dreams told us they were.

In my dream I trail as close to silence as words
allow, when they first attempt to chalk,
after its departure, the body's outline. I woke,
but no daytime could repair its monochrome.
Sunlight struck sacred and trifling plots
at the same time: my poetry books stacked
like mail trashed on the night table,
obscuring a hodgepodge of photographs.
In my eulogy's wake still roared a double silence
for the body's two bodies: my dead father
in a dream. And my dead father.

Wild Strawberries

Finches in the clothesline post
fall silent as I make my way along
the ground, the coiled vines,
mulch, dead sticks strewn
among darkening ground cover.
A groundhog comes this way
after crawling slowly, unafraid,
over the yard like a mist doing
its abracadabra over a lake.
Honeysuckle, black raspberry,
and wild grape sag from the fence.
Limbs smashed from the hurricane
prop against vines, and, paying
no mind to that past, green
and tender, they reach to begin
coiling up dead bark. I rip and saw,
lift armloads of viney green
to the fence and lay it over.
I wonder how last week's doe
made the thicket melt, her white tail
a flat hand as permanently trite
as a waving beauty queen's. I decapitate
pokeweed, slash that sham bigness,
throw it on top of a wall of trash.
Here and there poison oak
shoulders through: haughty,

overripe—a road company soprano—
expanding under the auspices
of pecan, cherry, and fir, whose
interposed limbs thwart its union
with sunlight. A finch
squawks from the trash pile,
making a big deal of my notice.
I work my way closer to her chicks
packed into their iron tube.
Through a day lily I can see her
wrenching in melodrama,
and I know I crouch in violation
of her express rules, a Caliban
who spreads his shadow through
the state-space of another's ecstasy.
Over my shoulder bees and bugs
dart, mercurial, through cylinders
of light. Others plunge entirely
into faces of flowers or rumble
through loam. A worm
awakened by a hoe blade
stirs like the time-lapse
of a tendril too young to name.
The possum lurks somewhere who
grimaced in the headlights.
Bats sleep in their cupboard,
undisturbed by the family
of squirrels on patrol from their drains,
tending to outrage, and trigger-happy

when the boorish bluejay swells nearby.
Consonant with every quickness,
whether it stays or goes,
they occupy a rotted corner
where, below and cool, skunks
sleep, who fear for nothing—
a queen and her sable kittens.
More limbs to come down,
more sticks and briars
to pluck and drag, strangling
weeds to find and root up
so that the wild strawberries
get a chance to offer up their
plump rubies before they perish
from contact with the earth,
like apples and peaches,
whole sides that lay there,
spoiling where you can't see,
complicit with their slow decay.
These are wasted utterly to air,
which is all fruition, blazing
where the light races, mashing
the world along its stupefying edge,
earth's edge, along which I creep.

Stefano

(dead in Rome, 2002)

Chianti and vodka. Porcini tossed
in steaming cords of pasta.
Everyone who came through the door was met
with your dash to the *cucina*,
wit countered with food,
class met by its isotope, style.
Hospitality proved everyone at length
an exile. It was your talent,
after years and worlds to equate
the walk-in with the friend,
the stranger with the family
you would not have. But houses
and habitués were your line:
to each an assignable place.
Your job and life merged more neatly
than the bratty painters and poets
gobbling the spreads at your famous parties
before swarming the corners where
some spidery countess or other still held court.
In that world of casual, contrived
rendezvous you found sweet order

a Wilde would have admired,
dancing mask-to-mask, who
were otherwise a long-ago injured child
nauseated by the turning of the knob,
parents' return, the grinding of keys.

Umbrian Odes

in memory of Joseph Brodsky

I.
Stacked stone holds its cutout against the blue.
Old window arches are bricked, having
been first covered with concrete
and that slagged off. Swallows loop
from cracks to air and back, and pigeons
perched like gargoyles gentle into sleepy,
perishable sentries. What is looked at persists
as the seen, in archaic recirculation.

Was this the old structure of the world—
to rise skyward on the sturdy back of matter?
Or was the ambition less, the organized
rubble only keeping pace with bodies?
As it happens, we are sitting by a pool
discussing cloth's impersonations of flesh.
While I like the indolence of silk, you
like the thing itself, even when it is

the shirt stuffed, a movement container.
The bald, smoking father orders
his cowed girls around the water. Enough
of the centurion survives his linteled brow
and granite nose to explain more

than towers, but he seems out of place,
subdued by his offspring's *gaucherie*,
as if the facial bearing were indifference's

rebuttal. A boatload of Darwins
could not console him for the arrival
of the rich couple and their aquiline,
disheveled children whose nearly
rotted innocence alerts the pornographer's
instrument. He knows they are closer
to stone than he and quick to assume
the *castelli* for their backdrop needs.

You hint that silk is a good thing because
it forces one to admit that violence
begets taste, if only that to pose words
in the manner of our sentience is to have
left capriciously on a long journey.
Like lying on our deathbeds, I add.
At which point, the pool takes, like
Narcissus, heaven's emptiness for itself.

II.
In sunlight, the landscape reverses Corot :
the front field of vision bright,
a hillside of attentive sunflowers, followed
by some darker stand of green—what life
summer puts in the way of life: ennui
of leaf-weight! An unstruggling tangle of grass

promises the skink to go with the hare.
Summer cancels and dispenses indifferently,
as the artist knew, who framed golden clearings
from the nearer embrace of indistinct

branches sedged with bitten leaves
and spotted fruit—Romantic props for a time
when selves let nature interrogate their
obscurity, wondering when the ball of gnats
would land or whether two sizes of viper
supported the theory that lower phyla
traveled *en famille*. Impossible, then, to turn
the sunflowers away from an allegory
of sunflowers, to resist thinking that
such doughty sunlight belonged to the past

and that things tightened up a bit once
the creek marked the sloping field's edge.
Perhaps old fields were always in the business
of leading the eye to the edge of the page,
after a sleep of fantastic flowers—
that felt you were watching them
through the page's tiny bars, and the change
that came over your face was like
a cloud that drifted behind your blown hair
and set by the roof of the old toolshed.

III.
Plow and harvest over the dead

and summer sunlight falling straight.
This, and the yolk competes with the fields
of sunflowers standing precisely at salute
until their fingers curl, but not the yellow.
The hog's destiny resembles the poem's,
in its way superior to the empty churches
watched over by the local police.

Fruits swell faster than a cloud.
Better to let them spot and fall, food
for wasps and inchworms making an alphabet
through their alimentary canals. Like paratroopers
peas strap-hang the whole length of July,
and when wheat exits via the dirt road
beside the beheaded grass, an owl is in
no better position than the useless twig

a canopy covered for. Gnawed by beetles,
sooted by harvest's systematic monsters,
a broadleaf sallies forth into Diesel air:
everywhere the same leaf claims its solar
privilege upon mountainous racks of the dead,
so sturdily inanimate that no question
can ever break through to the obtuse skulls
of the unfallen animals. But a farmer

sits in his cab as the truck pulls round
with its gaping hopper. Trailed by swallows
and a floating wake of dust, he pauses

DAVID RIGSBEE   163

to wipe the rearview mirror, his hand
extending to the window of the beast,
returning to cradle his own jaw that houses
his toothache, while his colleagues look on
and finish the lunch, that turns into siesta.

IV.
Trees and hedgerows, like an ink trail,
rewrite the hills into that realistic novel,
Joseph, you wondered the last century had missed.
Of the three segments of a vodka bottle, the first,
alone, seems incapable of bestowing poetry. Three
balls of gnats juggle for the favor of an apricot tree.
The local group, a few feet before my face,
give both force and nuance to the evening breeze.
Doves start up behind me, intoning
the bare syllable of their stony comfort.

A blue bus negotiates the road to town,
in which the cappuccino keeps dendrites
from drooping into winter kudzu.
Neither is the white car put off by geology.
The spiral up holds no improvement, save
the way down, etc. Consistency beats out surprise
in land, as in cuisine, eliminating any shadow
that would streak the yolk. Say what you will,
the mind pulls back from the brink in time
to switch either Tyson or Titian for Lucy.

Every day the Duomo tower indicates nothing
but diversifying clouds pulling back to reveal
a sky depopulated of everything save more clouds
and the occasional raptor touring emptiness
like Satan savoring the chaos. The wasp felt
a reassurance, that bare thermal pillar,
though once the grub's aspirations ranged across
the sexy fuzz of a peach. Epic vacillations
require hexameters designed to scythe
any shape that comes down the pike.

As for us, our best lines lie in canceled stanzas,
no doubt, homogenized by a silence as thick
as ennui. Let the thought, like a grub, climb out
the tops of our peach fuzz, for otherwise,
how keep past vividness from sinking to a level
that lets mediocrities step forward as maestros?
Existence merely arrived, Parnassian, but not
Parnassus. Still, a few molecules peeled from
the aqueduct, and pretty soon the whole Empire
faded before the more ancient snow of a television.

V.
When I turn, you are gone,
and it doesn't matter if I specify
the number of chairs, or simply
imply a renewed brightness around
the edge of the pool. No one observes
the mirror held to heaven. The sun

DAVID RIGSBEE   165

is having to work today, gesso
clouds refigure portions of sky.

Soon the whole. Meanwhile, I have
identified the dry sound, something
between a chitter and a buzz, by which
grasses hold forth when light eases.
A grasshopper, like a sprinter in his blocks,
kicks one hind leg into motion,
is answered by another enthusiast
not bound by sight, elsewhere in the yard.

In the distance, elemental thunder
expounds its critique against the eye's
regime, the regime of Piero and Cimabue,
who understood that the spectacle
of the hanged man secured meaning,
which is to say, proportion and difference,
crossing the retinal threshold to take
up residence in the soft place of matter.

Now, amphibian belchings intersect
but don't combine with birds' litanies.
My daily interventions inchworm across
the paper's flatland on their way to you:
but how oblique still, to the daisy's silent,
unmediated thrust that takes it a little bit
toward the sun, after having shouldered
its stuff above the paving stones.

Never Forget

A standard dove would gargle
all day, gnats dangle their pulsing clusters
like water-balloons. And the ground
be overrun with ants and scarabs
rearranging the earth. Figs
about to touch ground from the most extended
branch would note
how the necropolis corrects dissolution
with architecture. How domes
rewrite hills, and fields, grown and cut,
reduce the river's pull
where gravity is quietest and most
conspiratorial, a drift
content that a single painter restore it
from allegory to realism. Clouds
would process their variations
across the countryside all day.
What both bird and butterfly did would go
by the same name. And that ecstasy
pouring from the stone would pass
through wheat's variations,
when the mower appeared mounting the hill,
its red dome and puff of smoke
so like the scythes of the painters.

Into the Wall

An anvil-shaped cloud
spreads its iron shadow
across the hill adjacent to our town.
As on a floor viewed upside down,
other clouds, in turn, suggest
figures of the moment,
requiring only the arrival
of the next bit of future to cancel
the suggestions. The struggle
is ancient: clouds' agon drives the painter
into the wall, attempting impossible
compressions proper to time beyond
a lifetime. Here, where the sound
of a scooter merges with a wasp's nest,
a pack of flies beats up a swallow—
until the next frame. Or the classical
head turns with its look
of a god disappearing into time:
things are as they are,
turning in middle air,
and as they will be,
emerging from the rock.

Vespers

Wind carries off the slighter
birds, after which a purling of doves
adjusts the evening. An owl stands
quiet as a pine cone when a blade of light
breaches the hilltop and is gone. Behind me,
a compact car carries compact profiles
to town. Only a cloud, like a lipstick kiss
left on a mirror, offers
its supplemental farewell to the unbroken haze.
This is the final atmosphere
of a work day, not great bindings
but the modest affinities: bread
crossing the table,
as the jet engine overcomes the dove.

Houses in a Necropolis

Pretty huts, cells of memory:
these dead were not put by
but elevated. The cloud's shadow
must first climb the walls,
then inch up and over wavy roofs,
unlike the scything sweeps of light
on a grave. The stone believes
the future is repetition, desirable
in itself, a hill as matrixed
and parceled as any Cézanne,
where the seasons roll unimpeded.
The stone encasing the star-
tilted skeletons knows the ochre
and browns and the limiting cases—
yellows and purples, as well as trees
and bushes, Germanic, obeying orders,
whether in forests or trimming
a cathedral's ground to secure
in nature what a Trinity of chairs
could not, dulled by dust, or bursting
into flames. The stone is also the vault
from which the past cracks
its coffers, and the dead claim
neither justice nor business has
the same length as life, even as they
reach to lock in the embrace.
The stone is also the vault.

Not the Tall Grass

Even spotted with sarcomas, leaf-mold,
egg-cases, and the clean-bore holes
left by complacent worms, the fig tree
sees to its own dead indiscriminately
with a seam's load of fruit.
Mounting sun-warmed church stones
miles away one could rise to
apertures to locate spirit's participation
where green bounded green, and a hill
became plural. For on one side
bars of rain advanced on the promontories,
announced by sticks of lightning;
on the other, a field of sunflowers
like lungs before diving, stood
at fullest bloom for miles. We
came to affirm an identity in stone—
doves' headquarters, our
decoration—until earth could yield a second
figure equal to our mass, as granite
and marble trimmed the spirit with irony,
and the eyes could be startled again
there, where the mower stopped.

Qua

Foreground: wheat close up
and the morning's birds. Doves
packed in stone chatter brilliantly.
Background: gauzy, not much help.
Hills are nets, each node a village.
By the Cinquecento, the mariner myth,
like the bookish shepherd who lugs
a sacked lamb across the landscapes
of countless murals, had set in: time-
as-sea, as much time as a net lets pass,
until waves rise up into question marks
before rolling on to find, everywhere,
stony coast materializing from mist.
And sea-as-*si*, that term of assent, that
agreement—so long in coming—to let
stones take the place of waves.

Mowing Day

Just when grass dreams it isn't wheat,
over a rise, like Hannibal's elephants,
combines begin gouging road-width
channels through a meadow.

Midsummer, mid-morning.
Fallen clouds still hug the river,
reluctant to join the cirrus stream
challenging a distant vapor trail

(though both directions stand
to benefit from the transaction).
Gone to seed, the wheat's a brass
plaque offered to one hillside

by another, itself eclipsed by an acre
of no-longer-Impressionist sunflowers.
Machines whose grunting fools
only sparrows, sweep all before them,

iron tusks bobbing, leaving only
a shimmering insect circumflex
floating over the cropped layers
and swifts glutted on the radiance

surrounding stone. But all's rising

DAVID RIGSBEE   173

until clouds become a vertical field
where ground and sky take out their maps
and get down to gesturing and pointing.

174   THE RED TOWER

Secret Hours

Like an equestrian act, a cloud
swivels, turns inside out, then rights
itself crossing Roman air space.
In the picture, Montale sits at a window,
smoking. Terrace candles,
in sympathy, blow smoke into
the air above the street. Appearance
distinguishes the party at Stephen's.
Will the Borghese come? The Agnelli?
Dr. Johnson said people were right in
public to prefer a duke to a genius
(though in secret hours they were
also right to steal off to please themselves).
Over the terrace, down in the street,
scooters streak by the methadone clinic.
In the next room, a fantastically tall
woman lifts a melon cube to her lips.
Her head is ringed with acanthus leaves.
A poet is forced to deliver the story
of his life in dreamy self-parody.
Like a bid at cards, his "I was there,"
washes away, as wine does,
what the past itself has failed to do.
Smoke blows over the lip of the terrace.
Montale is looking out the window,
where a lizard's push-ups
lose count of acts and silences.

Terra Cotta

The little bird outpaced the bigger bird
and it seemed for a minute
it would turn and attack.
But summer was well under way
and aerials reclaimed the airspace.
This life—half arboreal, half slab—
waits to give eyes what is denied
to bodies: a place to land that has
no memory of the pain of landing.
Terra cotta softens balconies' iron.
Stucco turns sunlight decorative,
a series of hues that funnel eyesight
to open doorways where shadows
take over the domestic space
in the name and shape of light.

Air Traffic

Even at mid-morning, a cock-crow
lacerates the valley air. Bees swarm
under the eaves, bypassing a watermelon
and sugar bowl well within reach.
As durable as one of Ulysses' men
the old artist heads for his shed,
chisel in hand. His granddaughter forgets
the scorpion sweep under the bed that set
her teeth chattering half the night.
Her days are as rich as a French duke's,
an inventory of pranks and schemes
canceling the past's sensational void.
Today's air traffic, which is all duty,
seems all play, a general dalliance
that retreats to the open for cover.
Invisibility swallows a helicopter,
and modernity mutes the church bells
whose benediction too hangs in air
too short a time to become a soundtrack,
but long enough to cleave the day
into halves, with *then* falling flat
as a paving-stone, and *thereafter*
standing with its sheer face glistening.

Scenes on an Obelisk

The people across raise the flag of their laundry.
A cypress blocks St. Peter better than atheism.
Little bits of animation link up
into archipelagoes: beetles are the traffic
up and down a trunk, the trunk forking
in time to wave alike over a passing car
and rooftops of bulrush aerials.
All that was spirit seems naturalism
caught in the light.
A cross-dressed monk feeds the poor
cats of his block from a can.
Their satisfaction leaves them mild
for the morning, as he slips behind
a human-dwarfing door, exchanging sunlight
for a dark hallway's eroded slate,
and the darkness takes him
before the perspective does.

Such as Stone

A man on the pavement sweeps
dust down an incline, "the dust cure,"
someone calls it, as more behind him
rises from a construction pit,
getting a ride from windshields and farings.
The silhouette of an old woman
framed more delicately than a Giotto
becomes the profile of a sink
which flares, in turn, into a sunburst.
Thus did mannerism acquire a bad name,
but not among pots and pans
nor a porch's *disjecta membra*—
urns, ladder, hoses, tables—
for which regulation is greeted
with the inert's equivalent of a shrug.
Nor among pigeons whose sameness
imposes upon nothing, taking nothing
as text. Rooting among tiles,
bobbing under cars, they almost remember
their squeaky pinions' logical finale.
But of escaping stone there is no end,
nor of finding it where air would be,
the lofty reaches, where a little dust
scouts the spaces, doing what air does
when speech and exhalations
move it off the stone.

The Digs

An archaeologist said the garden paintings
were preserved when the building collapsed.
We were moving into a new phase
like an industrial plant or an ordinary
moon. The queen was late twenties—
already old, already mother to a child
grown big enough to weather a dynasty.
We stood on either side of a new trench
and heard how the hanging gardens
descended all the way to the ground level
of a distant past; how she could see
the capital from her country villa.
Useful, too, when her new husband
wished to visit—but keep an eye on things.
The garden paintings that brightened her
when she walked underground were now
the glories of the state museum. In sorrow,
in quick surprise, I saw the two figures
of women on either side of Pluto's garden
joined at the brink, while butterflies
of that pale field above *caput mundi*
probed oleander and fled the stone.

End of Sight

At first I thought of the leaves:
soon only backlit, except for streetlamps'
ambient blank. But then I noticed
cars moving between trees
and on the next block, porch lights
and lighted windows half given
over to blinds. Finally the last
in the harvest of lightning bugs—
just one or two, really, like tugboats
into some depth (once a regression
of poppies swallowed by the infinite)—
went out in time to draw the ear in
to the soughing of the treetops
and a private plane somewhere,
invisible, tugging its weight.
And that pulled the eyes after it, up,
beyond the darkened green to the smooth,
featureless presence of the sky,
until they were finally on their own
and useless at the same time,
as if the end of sight were
the point of sight.

from *Cloud Journal*

Where is the cardinal who set his flame
below the window as I sat with a book
of old poetry like a Kevlar vest or hook
badging a veteran's lapel instead of a name?
And where is the rat who votes against home,
slithering over dirt piles under the porch?
Reading from a nose-script, inching with the torch
of his own pupils, pellets show the way he came.
But not why. My mentor would imagine the exact
words needed to get from beginning to end
of a line of verse. Translation was his votive
offering, an ideal world always razed by fact.
So plausible readings replaced fluency to mend
meanings, and then the deep green fuse of motive.

◆

The sky's hairdo reminds one of those
pewter biddies sitting in the waiting room,
their powder-blue Buicks marked for doom
lined up, grill after grill, as if close
enough to rescue them from the pose
they assumed, having survived the refurbished bloom
of a perm-and-set and spun from the loom
of second chances, wandered out with heightened nose.
Reduced to irrelevancy by sunlight
they unravel and take leave with a flourish

of vapors moving aside to reveal the show:
that blue, in turn, making way for night
whose Kollwitz charcoal made the colors vanish,
salmon slapping less hard each twist and blow.

◆

The mountains are out today, and the air
has the faded shimmer of air through binoculars.
The weather begs report like the memoirs
of a man to whom life has seemed unfair.
And yet, the categories don't declare
how feeble the wish to argue particulars
in the drone of airplanes and whine of cars
(but how round the weather in the glare
of summer sunlight). Midsummer's approach
puts mind in view of meridians, as if
time harrowed drama as well as trees,
leaving less and few and out-of-reach
what once was both individual and massive,
if only to cull and correct the histories.

◆

The flats of houses and spires of firs—
hillsides endure their human disturbance,
hives and organisms in all-night dance,
grotesque, methodical, but no worse
than classical authors in whose verse
hard pins down soft with sword and lance,
asserts and expands its circumference

before feeding on itself, to die of a curse.
Extrapolations that kill a poem can be
nevertheless true. A Japanese willow
accuses Euclid with long, irregular finger
from which a sparrow has flown to see
how intricate the green layers in multiple row,
in long branches where the evenings linger.

◆

Where the hummingbird sleeps my murder
is atoned for: invisible repose is the thing.
The lurid nightmares of Mother's last spring
lie down in a flower pot in centripetal order
like frieze-petals, while below the border,
a little rat tests the patio ring—
rank tail, whiskered snout sniffing—
a hunched coke-head trolling the French Quarter.
Three sparrows and a low-slung robin
vie for fountain space—all striving and fuss,
and now space signals the all-clear.
Such dreams play escort down the dead-end.
There is no calming the pronouns—I, her, us.
Does light rest, if beauty begins in fear?

◆

Fighter jets scream over in duck formation.
After the Fourth: Scarlatti,
Mother waiting at the foot, and the dead free.
Even years ago houseflies moved to their station

circling a chandelier in looping motion.
My grandmother spread out on the settee
mulberry-red, sweet as a manatee,
presided asleep over all our celebration.
The backstory cocks its unnoticed frame
and drops from sight as another wave
of aircraft in rapid formation flies
horizon to horizon where the same
windows wait, each deep as a forest cave
or silo, after corn, where childhood lies.

from *Sonnets to Hamlet*

The rasp of crows spreads along the sky,
each fresh surge a makeshift marker
birds make up, through which they glide
moments later like wit through a letter
when words make their nomadic way
across a page's sense-resistant desert.
Poor south, still and ever about to be
that page, opting for the discount version
of self first and then of place, schooled
to set things apart, to cloak coercion,
to see, before they burn, factories retooled.
I remembered Southwell's babe. In that version,
Everyman and Christ merged in poetic last breath:
no upgrade for the Savior, but a plus for death.

◆

Could I not have caught the burning oil?
The hand makes a vessel soon enough.
When the suicide hoists the silent barrel
to his soft temple, am I then too rough
a being to sense the click a continent's length
away? Away. The hand in sweeping points
to a grassy hillside where the knotted strength
of five men gone to ground with cracking joints
could not force one dirt crumb to give up
its earthly allegiance. Guilt pins its shadow-cape

to my posture made poor by pushing the cup
back across the table to my willing ape,
who can never hurt for what he doesn't feel,
tapping hard earth with his padded heel.

◆

Soon after the fire, long days of rain,
draperies unmoving in dark Victorian rooms
with silk tassels and clouded plaster stains.
In the distance, occasional thunder booms.
The strap-hanging, leaf-drooping water drop
replaces fire's *consummatum est*,
challenges the stone directly, rots the crop
dilutes a tincture, dissolves a nest.
The sound of continuous rain is not unlike
that of fire, but muffled, alluvial,
able to overwhelm, but unable to strike,
its method erosion, its path arterial.
Rain on a window knows the tenant's gone,
makes its way to ground and buried bone.

◆

I lie, but without waiting. That storm
of a distant day blew down my bones,
fed my brain through the canal of the worm
piecemeal, cemented my ear to clef-tones.
Time and cloud alike sweep by above
the humidor of skull from whose space
no neuron travels a pilgrimage of love,

DAVID RIGSBEE   187

no eyebeam penetrates the flap of face
still demurely sheeting the stubborn bone.
The "I" tears loose, begins a drift
not unlike the spools of smoke blown
that merge with cloud cover and lift
the last prayer-wave, like a rising pitch,
to blue, while body works the ditch.

◆

There is no inwardness like this:
floor after human floor collapsing,
pipes and fittings, miles of artifice
melted into the original mash of being,
selves exiled into the surrounding wood
like stuttered jokes, revenants with no more
ability to nourish than perishable goods
miles from the hungry. The locked door
stands guarantee to the role of matter.
Smoke like an idea's shadow occupying
all the room, shelves sway and shatter.
Wind going after is like the body's dying
into the body of a growing text,
each story pressing rapidly over the next.

◆

One foot on fire-ant dirt, and the mound
seethes, as the tiny warriors spread
a teeming liquid shadow over the ground,
jealous ghost, certain sponsor of the dead

were he to appear. He? It is genderless
as an avalanche, indifferent, wild to plunder.
The image of fire yanks me from my dress.
I would be, though dead, defender.
Webbed in crows, cured, my sternum-shield
earth-ripped, enemy of consummation.
Leaving the bone-case, rot-peeled,
I would move directly to my station.
Some of fire would fill me to the good
if, in my inwardness and death, I stood.

◆

A cloud's sponge sweeps the lawn from green
to other green: it's time come to scrub
the dead from the living surface, until, unseen,
utterly past, nothing is itself a hub
whose torque mills distances beneath its track.
Those antiworlds: trailing off, their banners
proudly bearing the non-colors through the icy black
of those eternities the faithful make their manners.
One could feel them as a child in church.
Years later, haunted by the solstice-sweep,
one feels their radar's ghostly blips that match
exactly the curve of leaf-fall, the salmon-leap.
The eclipse sped over the weaves, accounts say,
and as the sun died, scythed mountains like hay.

◆

Morning. Red in the flag, like hummingbird sugar,
seems ten parts water. The sky, Oxford blue,
makes a photo-op of things that beggar
description. Chairs propped in, dispelling dew,
suggest gatherings accomplished, or to come.
Their tables await a tent and washcloth to sweep
a nighttime's worth of shade-tree gum
and spiders' glassy cables bridging the deep
between chairs. Under a lawn cropped close
as a Marine sergeant's hair, earth
lies complacent in gain, which is our loss,
and crumbled folderal, which was our worth.
Sight moves to seeming from what was seen.
A sudden storm sweeps the terrace clean.

Notes

Four Last Songs. Richard Strauss, *Vier Letze Lieder* (*Four Last Songs*), based on three poems by Herman Hesse: "Früling" ("Spring"), "September," and "Beim Schlafengehen" ("Going to Sleep"), and Eichendorff's "Im Abendrot" ("Evening Glow"). Excerpts of these poems are capitalized.

"Since he is silent, do not lose this chance, but speak . . ." and "strange trees," *Inferno*, XIII, 80-81.

" . . . the goddam Mystical Rose," see H. Phelps Putnam, "Hasbrouck and the Rose,"

"cling to the walls of silence," see Max Picard, *The World of Silence* ("Illness, Death and Silence").

from *Sonnets to Hamlet*: On September 3, 1991, a fire in the Imperial chicken processing plant in Hamlet, North Carolina killed twenty-five people, predominantly single, black females, and injured fifty. Fire doors at the plant had been padlocked to prevent theft. Though most were found dead clumped around the fire door, another group escaped to the freezer where they quickly froze. Imperial Foods produced nuggets for Shoney's, Wendy's and other fast food restaurants. Hamlet, running along the pine woods and sandhills next to the South Carolina border, is the birthplace of jazz saxophonist John Coltrane.

About the Author

A native of North Carolina, David Rigsbee is the author of seven full-length collections of poems and has published critical works on Joseph Brodsky and Carolyn Kizer. He is co-editor of *Invited Guest: An Anthology of Twentieth Century Southern Poetry* and has been the recipient of fellowships and prizes from the National Endowment for the Arts, the National Endowment for the Humanities, the Virginia Commission on the Arts, the Fine Arts Work Center in Provincetown, the Djerassi Foundation, and the Academy of American Poets. He is contributing editor to *The Cortland Review*.